CLEAR YOUR CLUTTER
WITH Kate EMMERSON

CLEAR YOUR CLUTTER
WITH Kate EMMERSON

Live light, Live large

A practical, no-nonsense book that teaches you the **WHY** and the **HOW** of ridding yourself of emotional, physical and body clutter

www.metzpress.co.za

Join Kate's communities of support and inspiration

I have created a unique, private Facebook group for you. Once your request to join it has been approved, you'll be able to share your inspirational stories, insights and trials, get expert help from Kate and be supported by others on a similar journey. This group will help you to ditch your glitch and shift your life so that you can live light, live large.

To join the group, mail my team on shift@kate-emmerson.com and put "Request to join clear it" in the subject line. I will also send you all of the worksheets contained in the book.

There are plenty of ways to stay in touch with me:
www.facebook.com/kate-emmerson.page
www.kate-emmerson.com
Twitter: @kate_emmerson
LinkedIn: www.linkedin.com/in/kateemmerson

....

Published in 2013 by
Metz Press
1 Cameronians Avenue
Welgemoed, 7530
South Africa

Copyright © Metz Press 2017
Text copyright © Kate Emmerson
Cover photograph by Filmalter

All rights reserved. No part of this publication may be reproduced, stored in a retrieval system or transmitted in any form or by any means, electronic, mechanical, photocopying, recording or otherwise, without the prior written permission of the copyright owners.

Publisher: Wilsia Metz
Designer: Liezl Maree
Copy editor: Sean Fraser
Proofreader: Francie Botes

PRINT ISBN: 978-1-920479-68-8
POD ISBN: 978-1-928376-27-9
EPUB iSBN: 978-1-928376-25-5

To BP – For everything, always!
Your belief in me ensures I seek to BE more.

Day 1 – Preparation guidelines   67
Day 2 – Bedroom (Part 1)   74
Day 3 – Bedroom (Part 2)   76
Day 4 – Bathroom   79
Day 5 – Body, purse and handbag   83
Day 6 – Wardrobe (Part 1)   86
Day 7 – Wardrobe (Part 2)   91
Day 8 – Body   93
Day 9 – Kitchen (Part 1)   99
Day 10 – Kitchen (Part 2)   102
Day 11 – Books and magazines   105
Day 12 – Music   107
Day 13 – Memory lane   110
Day 14 – Living space   112
Day 15 – Dining room   115
Day 16 – Office or study (Part 1)   116
Day 17 – Office or study (Part 2)   121
Day 18 – Office or study (Part 3)   125
Day 19 – Body and car   126
Day 20 – Your choice!   129
Day 21 – That big area   135
Day 22 – Shifting to emotional clutter   138
Day 23 – Honesty   143
Day 24 – Money! Money! Money!   145
Day 25 – Boundaries   147
Day 26 – Detox your inbox   149
Day 27 – Forgiveness   154
Day 28 – Setting up systems   162

Contents

Foreword 8
Acknowledgements 9

1 Introduction 11

2 Unpacking clutter 15

3 The mangled triangle of clutter 25

Physical clutter 26
Body clutter 27
Emotional clutter 27

4 The clutter creep 29

5 Facing your clutter demons 35

6 Why all the invisible fishing lines? 45

7 Creating space and moving forward 61

8 Let's do it – day by day 67

Further reading 173
Reviews 174

FOREWORD

Growing up, it would seem that many of the adults thought their job as grown-ups was to program and condition me. They'd tell me what they thought I should think, feel and believe. So, growing up, I learned, was about accumulating: other people's ideas and knowledge, accumulating responsibilities, collecting a variety of emotional baggage, physical possessions and material things. And we'd often call this being mature and grownup.

But accumulating so much is also very draining. There are times in our lives when we can only move forward by actually letting go.

So much of our energy is invested in holding on to things – ideas, clutter, concepts. This doesn't leave us much free energy to be creative, loving, happy and inspired.

Kate is the queen of helping you identify what no longer serves you. She is the Deva of supporting you in letting go of what is holding you back. In this great book, Kate gently and firmly takes you by the hand to inspire you to the possibility that you can free yourself and free your energy. Having inspired you, she then shows you how to get going and how to keep going.

Letting go doesn't meaning losing things but it does mean having a new relationship with things, so that you have them rather than them having you. Kate guides you to a new relationship with your stuff and with yourself. Let her be your friend, your guide and your advocate. Let her give you the loving kick up the bum you may need to take charge of your life and set yourself on a happier and freer trajectory. I have known Kate for several years and she walks her talk – she has a passion and an energy that is infectious. Read and be positively infected.

Best wishes
Nick

Author, leadership expert

London, November 2012

ACKNOWLEDGMENTS

As I finalize this book, I am sitting in the bush in the beautiful Madikwe Game Reserve in South Africa. Viki – my friend since we were 12 years old – and her partner call this magnificent place home and it has gifted me the rare opportunity to be still and to focus. I feel deep gratitude to be here at this time, away from the craziness that my city life often epitomizes.

I am indebted, too, to my Mastermind group – having my book in print and selling was the goal that I brought to the space. Mastermind has been both a challenge and an enormous source of inspiration to ensure my commitment to my own goals.

I have thoroughly enjoyed the process of working with Metz Press and the team to whom I was introduced through a series of interesting unfoldings. My gratitude also to Sean for immaculate editing and for our lovely connection right from the start.

To my incredible assistant Nicole, my VA (virtual assistant) and researcher *par excellence*! Working with her has been an enlightening journey to increased effectiveness, helping me to stick to what I know and love best as she weaves her magic through my life and work.

Thanks to all my incredible staff who have accompanied me on jobs as we get deep and personal inside homes and offices. It is a blessing to do this work. And a special note of thanks to Prayer!

My dear friend Nick Williams, best-selling author and mentor, who always believed that there was a book in me and who got me started on the process.

And a thank you to all my friends and family around the world who make my life as full and interesting as it is – you all know who you are. A special note goes out to my brave and courageous mum, Lesley, who continues to be a source of great inspiration to me.

Finally, and most importantly, I dedicate this book to all the brave, bold and courageous souls who have invited me into their lives to help shift them and their clutter. Whether supporting them in physically clearing out their homes, via cyberspace through my e-courses, inspiring them when invited to talk at functions, through written articles or Skype sessions – with your permission, it is *your* stories that are woven through this text, because I know you will inspire others with your courage to let go.

Clutter clearing is not easy, and requires the tenacity of a bulldog, but the delight and freedom of living light that is waiting just on the other side of the process, will have you skipping for joy as *you* learn how to *live light, live large*.

With blessings,

Kate

The Quick Shift Deva

Introduction

'It is preoccupation with possession, more than anything else, that prevents men from living freely and nobly.' – Bertrand Russell

Age 7. One trunk. One term. A system that was designed to work.

Boarding school provided me with a system for life that I feel privileged to be able to share with you, no matter where you are on your personal clutter journey.

In my memory of that time, my two elder brothers were 'sent' to boarding school. Being the youngest, and the only girl, I decided that fair was fair and that I wanted to go too, aged 7. Seriously. It was a bit of a personal wail in terms of, 'If they can go, why can't I?' While most other kids shudder at the thought of boarding school, my independent nature would not allow me to let go of the idea. And, in retrospect, I honestly think it boded well for my future, allowing me to learn to live by the rules that still serve me to this day.

I had no choice but to abide by the military-like precision of green knickers living with green knickers, towels folded neatly, bed made before showering, keeping toiletries in one small bag, nothing lurking under the steel-framed bed, evening wear hanging with evening wear, for example. It was all about 'like with like' – and it had to be neat. Precision neat. Each of us had half a cupboard and a small bedside table. Every morning as we left the dorm area we had to polish our shoes at the end of the passage. It was a simple system that worked. Pocket money was fastidiously controlled by Mama Matron in her little black book and we had to request funds every week for sweets from the tuck shop. We even had a knickers, hair, nail and hemline check. *Eek!*

For me, it was never worth stepping beyond the parameters and facing the wrath of Matron. Although our junior dorm matron was much loved for her gentle nature, she had tools at her disposal. When pushed too far, such as catching us talking after 'lights out' or transgressing other such rules, she would, with a harsh voice, send us down the dark, twisty stairs that led into the kitchen. As punishment, we had to stand with our noses touching the cold wall, listening to the scurry of mice in the kitchen and the demons playing tricks on our minds. Towing the line, being responsible and just doing the things that worked for the system was a much easier option for me. I confess I also liked the regularity of it.

So, right from the start, I was lucky in that I found it easy to fit into a system that worked for me. I was only allowed to take what would fit into my black metal school trunk, no extras. Clothing (three different outfits for day wear, nightwear and Sunday wear), toiletries and edible extras had to last me a full term, with one home visit. There was something amazing about having absolutely everything I needed, but nothing in excess. I really do feel, when I contemplate my life retrospectively, that it was a rare gift to learn at such a young age.

Everything had a place and a reason. I even learned to revel in helping the matron sort 'intimate smalls'. While all our main laundry (with neatly sewn-on name tags) was carted off-site weekly, all the girls' knickers and bras were done in-house. They would be laid out on long trestle tables in the 'undies' room, in alphabetical order. They had to be folded so that they'd fit within the name slot, and every night you had to collect yours so as not to let them build up and cause mayhem in the undies room.

Like many kids going through a phase, one of my favorite pastimes at primary school was collecting 'stuff'. Most girls did this simply as a way to add some element of amusement to what can otherwise be dreary boarding-school life and a way to connect with each other. 'Stuff' was things like beautiful writing-paper sets, exquisitely decorated with matching envelopes and a second, spare sheet, miniature perfume bottles (thanks to my mum, who was a pharmacist with regular access to the perfumery reps donning their wares every month), posters, glass animals and annual diaries. I even collected erasers, stickers and *Hello Kitty* goodies (which, I see, have made a huge comeback in recent years).

However, I also knew how to look after all my stuff, respect it and store it. I loved to look at it, see it, touch it, appreciate it and feel it – and often. I cherished the stuff I collected and knew their value would be retained (thereby giving me better bargaining power at school) by looking after and respecting them. My pride and joy was my writing-paper collection. At the beginning of term we would all arrive back with new additions acquired over the holidays, ready to get into the swap frenzy, demanding two or even three sheets of paper for one special collection. It also taught me the art of negotiation. My paper was to be envied, or so I thought, and I had it all sorted into categories so it was easy to find and ogle over. Duplicates were kept separate, as they became bargaining collateral. Oh the young entrepreneurial mind. It was all kept in my dad's old shirt boxes to ensure safe preservation. Long live paper!

My love of moving, traveling, seeing the world and experiencing exotic cultures ensured that after university I pretty much sold up all that I had to venture out into the world. I still live in this light way, free to pack up and travel light the moment an opportunity arises. As I explored and adopted a more spiritual way of living in my twenties, I learned to let go of the collections of 'stuff' I had once loved. Garage sales, boot sales, anything to off-load and lighten up so I could skip off to new exciting adventures. Traveling with my backpack once again emulated my black tin trunk at school.

Have only what you absolutely need, nothing in excess. My traveling rule was that I had to carry everything myself, and if I wanted to buy anything in the country I was visiting, I had to choose one precious item that would encapsulate the journey. I only detoured from that rule when I knew I was coming back home to South Africa, and used the last of my funds to buy up local jewelry in Bali to bring back and sell, so it was more of an entrepreneurial business opportunity intended to fund the next stage of my trip than pure indulgence on my part.

• •

Living light is the essence of who I am and what I aim to share so that *your* life is more meaningful, purposeful and focused on what truly matters. I honestly do not expect everyone to be a minimalist; it is not about being frugal or living in denial. It is about living with a lightness in your step because you have zero clutter – in all areas of life. It is about channeling your energy into the things that really matter so that you can focus and prioritize, rather than waste your precious time and energy on that which is sapping your spirit.

The world of clutter is one filled with shame, embarrassment, a lack of systems, being stuck in the past, living with diminished energy and never having enough time. It is all about feeling 'not good enough'. We all feel that we *should* know how to deal with our mess, disorder and excess, to let go and to forgive, yet often we just lose our way and need some additional support.

Are you ready to get stuck in, to learn about the three different, yet intertwined areas of clutter, and to have a step-by-step system to follow to finally get on top of your cluttered life?

Some things are best learned well from a young age. However, I unequivocally believe in the ability of adults, that means *you* – no matter how old, no matter how bad you think your situation is, no matter how hopeless and desperate it appears, to learn new habits. That is my aim, to help you rewire your ability to sort and order, no matter how cluttered your life might be right now.

In this book, you will learn to sift through all your clutter and adopt easy-to-follow systems once your clutter has been cleared. That is my promise to you. I have helped thousands just like you, with worse clutter habits than yours. There is hope. And plenty of it.

My gift is to be able to teach you the *why* and the *how* to get it done. When you understand why you have clutter, and have learned some simple tools and techniques, you will be sorting through all your 'stuff' in a jiffy. Clutter and hoarding are not new, but they have become a modern disease that is manifest in many forms. My wish is to clean up the world, one life at a time.

When you have understood the empowering definition of clutter in my world, you will be able to approach every single aspect of your life from a new angle, thus stepping into the fabulous energy of *living light, living large!*

Unpacking clutter

'Perfection is not when there is no more to add, but no more to take away.'
– Antoine de Saint-Exupéry

When you consider the clutter in your life and the reason you may have picked up this book in the first place, it is very likely that you were thinking about some of the following:

- Your messy desk
- Trash that needs clearing
- Clothes that don't fit
- Clothes you don't wear
- Stuff that is broken
- Unwanted gifts stashed in a cupboard
- Anything you're hanging onto 'just in case …'
- Old magazines or newspapers piling up somewhere
- That overflowing drawer, cupboard, room or garage
- Too many things in too small a space
- A general lack of organization
- Other people's stuff – dead or alive
- Sentimental knick-knacks
- 'Baggage' – of every variety …

Defining clutter

The dictionary definition of clutter is:

- *to strew or amass (objects) in a disorderly manner*
- *a condition of disorderliness*
- *to make a place untidy and overfilled with objects*
- *the mess created when too many things are in a place*
- *a state or condition of confusion.*

So while the dictionary version is a great start and does well to *describe* clutter, it does not offer the whole picture. We need to unpack this idea further. For our purposes, we require a more empowering definition. I would like to offer a definition that reveals a bigger picture, a bigger reason and a better understanding. If we step beyond the obvious, incorporate an understanding of the three different aspects of clutter and allow the definition to become a clue to moving beyond its grip, we can define clutter in more accessible terms:

Clutter is anything that no longer serves you, for whatever reason.

Please read that definition again. And again. And now ask yourself, 'What does this conjure up for me?'

This definition is all-inclusive, regardless of the shape or form clutter takes. If it is not adding any current value and no longer serving you in some way in your life, it is classified as *clutter!* Cool, huh?! Whether we are referring to outdated clothes, messy paperwork, limiting beliefs that clutter our mind or congested circulation in our bodies, we can now put all clutter under the same all-encompassing definition.

Having defined clutter, this now opens up your perspective of what it entails. Even if you feel that you are the neatest, most ordered and organized person, you can start to view your stuff (be it things, people or anything else) with a fresh perspective, and scrutinize it using this broader definition.

Go easy on yourself

This definition also lets you off the hook a little – because at some point your clutter did, and possibly still does, serve you. Perhaps the red dress that once grabbed attention from admirers; the gym equipment you bought and started using to shed those extra pounds; the papers that defined your life; the magazines that you bought in anticipation of inspiring ideas; the knick-knacks and antiques that beautified your home; the stuff you needed to buy when more people lived in your home; the friends who completed your life; the smoking habit you took up to help you feel more confident at parties in your twenties; the pain and illness or even excess weight you manifested to protect yourself; the shopping you did when not knowing how to deal with your emotions – all of that somehow served you in the moment, at *that* moment.

So the question, 'Does this serve me now?' is not about judgment, which merely exacerbates how bad you feel about yourself; it is not about whether your clutter is good or bad, valuable or trash, right or wrong, positive or negative, but simply about whether your stuff serves you *now* or not.

It is not about judgment, guilt, shame or blame. It simply means being in the present and evaluating everything and everyone in your life.

> **TIP:** It might be useful to take a break, grab something to drink and just sit quietly pondering this new definition to help you get a sense of where this concept fits in your world.

An invisible image of clutter

Allow me to paint a metaphorical picture: On the front of your body – about where your stomach lies, just between your rib cage, by your sternum – is the area known as your solar plexus, the place where we say we have 'butterflies' in our tummy.

Imagine that every single thing you are holding onto, things that no longer really serve you, has a thread of invisible fishing line that emanates from your solar plexus. And at the end of every single thread of fishing line is a very big, heavy, glass bottle filled with lead. Clutter, literally and figuratively, weighs you down:

- Keeps you stuck
- Heavy
- Stagnant
- In the past
- Unable to jump into your future
- Too tired to see the present moment.

Now imagine finding the right scissors and snipping all those invisible fishing lines and releasing the lead weights. Wow, what an instant freedom and lightness of being you will experience!

By the time you have completed this book and done all the step-by-step exercises, you will be as light as a feather, ready to face your world with gusto.

Expanding humans

Our destiny as humans is to evolve. We are designed to expand into the best version of ourselves that we can possibly be. We need to look for things that prevent us from taking this journey.

> 'Everything you want is just outside your comfort zone.' – Robert Allen

It really is worth taking the time and making the effort to discover the underlying cause of why you gather, collect, harbor, cling to and generally hoard stuff.

If 'it' is not adding value to your life *today*, then it is time to haul yourself into the present moment, deal with all the reasons why you are holding onto it, and be willing to let go. The process requires trust and faith. When letting go in any area of life, we always fear the worst – what if nothing or no one else comes my way, what if I regret my decision today? But the energy it requires to hold on to the old is detrimental to embracing the new. Rather than waiting until you have to be pulled kicking and screaming into a new era, why not let yourself do it consciously and willingly? There can be grace and elegance in that.

Legacy

One simple fact – if you do not teach yourself to let go of anything that no longer serves you now, then one day when you die you will leave your mess and chaos for your loved ones to clean up. Do you really want to do that?

Imagine making your family or friends go through all your stuff, or worse yet knowing they are just throwing it all away because they can't deal with it? If you can't be bothered to respect it, then why should they? Or perhaps they simply do not know how to and will call in someone like me to do it on their behalf. So all that stuff you're holding onto – it's time to sort it out.

Perhaps you are so bogged down with emotional clutter that you don't know how to get started on your physical clutter. Or, subconsciously, you might even want to punish other people. In reality, however, you're only punishing yourself by not giving yourself the opportunity to live light again. I get calls all the time from people who need my help to clear out a beloved's mess after their death. If you honestly treasure yourself and respect your life, and treasure the folk you might leave behind, then it's time to get it in order in every sense of the word and show yourself how much you truly care about yourself.

Leave your legacy well respected, preserved and in great order.

Modern lifestyles

Nowadays there is an incessant and ever-increasing demand on our time, space and energy, and we are constantly being pulled into it, often subconsciously. Our senses are bombarded by a barrage of information and technology, the smallness of the global village and the need to be connected 24/7. Unless we consciously take ourselves off the grid, adopt the concept of reduce, re-use and recycle, and take constructive steps to simplify our lives, then the hamster wheel of acquisition will take us on a helter-skelter ride to hell.

'One of the dangers of habitual accumulation is using the time available for enjoyment in furious acquisition of more and more. We substitute the joy of ownership for the desire of accumulation. Luxuries become necessities. The tyranny of things overwhelms the acquisitive heart.' – Fred Smith

So, unless you want to be crushed by your stuff, it's time to take stock and live with a sense of lightness.

● ●

As consumers, we are bombarded with *Buy! Buy! Buy!* The increase in the regularity of shops and businesses offering 'sales' to generate cash flow means that the temptation to buy is ever increasing. We are part of a world of consumerism that encourages purchasing way beyond our needs. Our world facilitates and indeed encourages debt, and promotes acquisitions of every description. This makes it difficult to keep our lives clear, up to date and clutter free. The advent of shopping online has also made it increasingly easy to acquire material goods 24/7 from the comfort of our couches, filling the gaps in our emotional lives with stuff.

Chilling figures from *Avoiding Future Famines* released by the United Nations Environment Program show that a third of food produced globally every year does not reach human mouths – it is either lost in transit or wasted by consumers themselves. This amounts to a staggering 1.3 billion tonnes every year. Even with over 9 million people starving, we still see statistics such as the fact that American consumers throw away 25% of all food they purchase, and British consumers discard roughly 33% of their purchased food due to factors such as over-purchasing in response to marketing offers. This highlights the problem of excess and accumulation without recycling or redirecting it where it needs to be.

On 14 September 2011, the UN Secretary-General Ban Ki-moon made the following remark at a special event to launch the '7 Billion Actions' initiative in New York:

> 'In just seven weeks, the global population will reach seven billion. We are not here simply to acknowledge that milestone. We are here to address all of its vast implications. The seven-billionth citizen will be born into a world of contradictions. We have plenty of food, yet millions are still starving. We see luxurious lifestyles, yet millions are impoverished. We have great opportunities for progress, but also great obstacles.'

If we take a moment to align ourselves to the world at large, we realize the same thing happens in our own lives: we often have an excess that trips us up at the expense of those who may have absolutely nothing, be it food, clothing, appliances, toys, equipment or linen. Imagine, then, getting rid of your clutter and, as a bonus, in the process transforming another person's life? Is that exciting or does it add to the overwhelming burden of, 'What am I going to do with all the stuff I no longer wish to keep?' There are charities in your area that will gladly collect the stuff you no longer need – they make it easy for you to pass your stuff on with just one phone call. I urge you to not allow yourself to be overwhelmed by this task. Focus your energy on clearing your clutter, then you can pose the question of how to distribute your goods in the online community. We will help you find someone in your area to come and collect.

●●●●●●●●●●●●●●●●●●●●●●●●●●●●●●●●●●●●●

You can make a difference in your own home, and clearing your clutter with my help is your starting point. Too many of us are still living with the notion that more is better, rather than reflecting on some important questions:

- What do I really need?
- What will actually add value to my life?
- Am I keeping the right things for the right reasons?
- Are my priorities in order?
- Is my home aligned to my values?
- Am I being the best possible version of myself the way I am living?

Imagine if you started focusing your energy on quality over quantity, purpose and fulfillment over accumulation. In many ways, we are being called back to a more conscious way of engaging with our life, our time, our value and our possessions. But that starts with *you* in your own home, your own desk, your own cupboard, your own body, your relationship with yourself and how you engage with others in the world.

Now is the time to …

- Stop buying duplicates simply because you have no idea where stuff is.
- Stop filling the emotional hole by amassing more stuff.
- Stop cramming your mental space with mess so that you have an excuse not to get on with your life and focus on what matters.
- Stop giving in to your kids or family by buying more stuff to make them happy and assuage your guilt.
- Stop trying to fill every ounce of time so that there is no space for your soul to breathe.
- Let go of the need to be constantly connected and wired up 24/7.
- Once and for all, stop running away from the real issues …

Instead, you need to consider the following:

- Start refocusing on what's important.
- Live with what and whom you love.
- Keep your life simpler so that you have more energy.
- Be brave enough to carve your own route rather than following the crowd of accumulators.
- Set up systems to make your home and life work more effortlessly.
- Start saying *No!*
- Start letting go of anything that no longer serves you.
- Start being honest in all your communication.
- Start honoring your body if you truly value your life.
- Start taking downtime off the social media radar in order to connect in the flesh with friends and family.
- Be willing to trust this process of clutter clearing and get to the other side.

In order to be inspired to do something constructive, we have to be conscious of clutter and its negative effects. If you are reading this, then you are on the right path …

Why clear clutter?

Letting go makes room for the fresh, the new, the exciting and the endless possibilities that lie ahead in the zone of clutter-free living. It increases our ability to show up and be fully present emotionally, engaged with our life, as opposed to being pulled down by the weight of those lead-filled bottles.

If we look to nature, we see a homeostatic system of flow whereby the natural world always endeavors to regain harmony; nothing in nature is ever stagnant, unless it has been interfered with by us humans. Perhaps there is a way we can look to nature to teach us about cycles and the natural ebb and flow that exists no matter what. It may serve us to emulate this aspect of our natural environment, and remember to let things go, pass stuff on and thus flow with all the different seasons of life.

We only have to look at the 'external' four seasons to be reminded of when to reap and when to sow. Our lives are very different in winter to summer if we tap into the natural demands of that time. We can also look at the cycles of the moon – since time immemorial, it has been accepted that the two weeks following a full moon is a time for letting go, of ridding yourself of things that no longer serve you. The new moon thus signals a calling of new things into our lives. Nature guides us to let go regularly.

We could also look at our 'internal' seasons – birthdays or anniversaries, for example – which are more in tune with our personal life. The new year or a religious festival may be a natural pivoting point for letting go. It can also be useful to think of the time just before your birthday as the symbolic season of winter (letting go, shedding and retreat) and getting ready for the growth of spring – a symbolic, personal 'new year' happens on your birthday, a great time to start afresh with the year ahead.

● ●

For all you shopaholics reading this, think about the psychology of what retailers are regularly doing by way of their 'sales'. The concept is threefold: firstly, they are tapping into the psychology that you are saving money by buying goods on sale; secondly, that you will feel as if you have missed out if you leave the items there; thirdly, they are traditionally making more space available for newer merchandise. After each season, we see big sales – letting go of the stock they no longer need that is taking up precious space in order to make space for the new items for *you* to buy.

The Common Sense Investor (http://csinvestor.com) says, 'It turns out that the biggest money mistakes in today's world come in the form of paying for things that you neither need nor get any real benefit from'.

The same principle applies to our daily hygiene when we use face cream, for example. You wash your face first, before putting your cream on. Imagine if, every day, you kept applying cream to your face without first removing the grime of the previous day … *yuck!* You would look awful, feel awful and probably come out in revolting spots. It would make sense to apply the same logic with every single area of your life too, and yet we battle to do it in our lives, don't we?

Nature constantly reminds us that we should be shifting naturally between different seasons, bowing to the ebb and flow, yet as humans, we tend to get stuck. We keep 'things' for too long and refuse to let go of people, places or habits in a timely manner. We cling on for as long as possible because we're generally scared of change.

We will delve more deeply into the reasons why we keep clutter in Chapter 5.

3

The mangled triangle of clutter

'The secret of all victory lies in the organization of the non-obvious.'
– Oswald Spengler

Using the definition of clutter as 'anything that no longer serves you, for whatever reason', let's now move on to the different categories of clutter, so we can gauge the full spectrum and understand how this triangle holds itself together in a mangled web.

Clutter is not confined to the physical mess or disorderliness as outlined by the dictionary definition. The three aspects of clutter are fabulous cohorts, intertwined at every twisted turn. Rest assured that when you start working on one aspect, it will have a positive cumulative effect on the next aspect, and so on. The triangle is simply different manifestations of a similar underlying cause.

In my twenties I was a professional aromatherapist practicing in South Africa. During this time, I developed a deep love and respect of the body and its ability to heal itself, as well as how our bodies create and store toxins. Through stress management, healing and meditation, I started understanding the process and effects of stress on our bodies.

The teachings in which I immersed myself taught me about the power of our spiritual aspect (regardless of our religious beliefs) and how we need to feel up to date and at peace in order for us to be present and powerful in our lives. Retrieving our 'spirit energy' from people and belongings from our past is vital to be able to live *now*. In my thirties I studied professional life coaching, coupled with Neuro-Linguistic Programming (NLP) and Emotional Freedom Technique (EFT). I was then able to expand my work and start supporting clients to shift emotional, spiritual and mental baggage in a practical way.

My lifelong ability and desire to *Live light, live large* led me to offer professional clutter-clearing services on a small and large scale, reworking whole lives and supporting whole families for total transformation. The stories of those brave clients are woven through the practical process outlined here to inspire you along the way.

These three areas of life are inextricably linked to each other if we wish to *let go of anything that no longer serves us*. Let's take a closer look.

PHYSICAL CLUTTER

Physical clutter is the tangible 'stuff' we can see, touch and feel in our physical world.

My fascination with how we store and retrieve stuff so that we waste not an ounce of energy or time looking for things, coupled with over 15 years of helping people at a physical level in their homes, has shown me that everyone dreams of living with their own version of order and practical systems. No one feels great about having physical mess, but all too often people are just too overwhelmed to know where to start – even if you were once the most organized person, life can and often does get in the way.

The physical clutter in our environment carries a lot of weight in our lives (in terms of both actual pounds and the real space that it fills around us). Every time you walk into a cluttered or messy room, sit at your full, paper-strewn desk or open your cupboards, you know that your mess and the resultant chaos are stealing precious energy from you.

Physical clutters fills actual space in your life so you do not have to feel or think. It includes clothes, books, CDs, toys, appliances, magazines, tools, car parts, newspapers, documents, food, toiletries and anything else that you can *see*. And yet it has a dire impact on how you *feel*.

BODY CLUTTER

Body clutter is anything that steals your va-va-voom and vitality.

Your body has several internal cleansing mechanisms designed to sweep your system clean. These systems of input and elimination are designed to nourish you and to rid your body of the excess you no longer require (blood circulation, lymphatic system, kidneys, liver, skin, bowels and lungs, for example). If you put the wrong things into your body and do not allow them to be efficiently eliminated, you are physiologically holding onto cellular stuff that no longer serves you. You are literally clogging up the space in your body.

Think about excess weight, cellulite, pain, illness, cancerous or other toxic cells, constipation, skin disorders, atherosclerosis – anything that is clogging you up, and stealing your energy and *va-va-voom*.

I am sure you can recall times when you were forced to deal with emotional pain or baggage or perhaps the reaction to walking into your chaotic home yet again, and feeling the way it instantly steals your vital energy and plasters you to the couch, only just able to flip through the TV channels with not another ounce of energy to spare.

EMOTIONAL CLUTTER

Emotional clutter cannot be seen – we can only experience the insidious effect of everything that keeps us playing small and steals our personal power by lugging around emotional baggage.

This category may seem nebulous, but it can be devastating in its negative impact. Remember the hundreds of fishing lines attached to bottles filled with lead?

This aspect of clutter takes up emotional, mental and spiritual space in your life, and thus drains or saps your energy, thoughts and time. It jeopardizes your ability to step up and step out in your life, to feel good about your body, to face the mess in your life. It consists of all that *yucky* stuff, such as the negative emotions we cling to: anger, resentment, guilt, betrayal, frustration, hurt, unfinished business, incomplete conversations, unpaid bills, and so much more.

Clients always ask, 'But where do I start?', with a look of terror in their eyes. 'Should I tackle my bedroom before my boss, my body before my living room?' It matters not, I answer, because they are all intertwined. All that matters is that you simply start!

You already have, by reading this far, so let's shift to the next step …

The clutter creep

'What you think about, talk about, and get off your ass and do something about is what comes about!' – Larry Winget

By the 'clutter creep' I'm not referring to a creepy person here, but rather the verb – the manner in which clutter usually appears in your life. It just creeps up out of nowhere, and then keeps seeping into all areas of your life.

Have you ever been to Singapore? Or experienced South Africa's Gautrain (the fast-track train service in Gauteng)? When there are rules of zero tolerance imposed on littering, it is quite easy to stick to the program and not deviate one iota.

In my early twenties I traveled to South-East Asia, and one of my stopovers was Singapore. What instantly struck me was how impeccable everything was: cleanliness and order throughout the city and all the public spaces. I remember being warned at the hotel about being very vigilant not to litter in any form or throw gum on the roads, as the consequences would be dire. It was incredible to be in such a beautiful, neat and respected space. It made it easy to breathe and to be.

And what about the rest of the Far East, where Feng Shui is commonly practiced? Feng Shui is the art of placing objects in the right place for the right reasons in order to create flow and harmony in a space, to benefit all who live there – everything has its place and is precisely ordered. The understanding of a bigger picture of flow and harmony to create ease of living means that everyone respects the space more. There is no place for clutter or litter.

In South Africa, where I am from, we for the most part face a huge challenge when it comes to litter: with many people living below the poverty line it means that food is their most important survival challenge. You can understand that being concerned for one's environment when you have nothing in your belly is not going to enjoy a priority. Discarded plastic shopping bags are scattered everywhere and many citizens generally disrespect the streets and their public spaces. It is common to see people throw trash out the windows at traffic lights.

Yet the new Gautrain simply operates according to different rules – zero tolerance for all. The first time I climbed aboard while chewing gum, the official marched me over to the trash can and told me to spit it out. I kid you not. As a result, this entire transport system is spotless, manicured and pristine.

Clutter is the same – when the environment is 100% clean and clear, you can spot one minuscule discarded wad of gum a mile off. Of course, the opposite also holds true. Think about it …

Clutter attracts clutter

Scenario. You drive your car into the garage and have to weave your way through piles of junk, scratching your car as you open the door; you walk into your home and at the front door you are greeted grimly by piles of stuff strewn carelessly behind the door; the kitchen is littered with dirty dishes, groceries, papers and packets, with no visible sign of kitchen counters. You take your food and drink to the living room, where the scatter pillows are rumpled, magazines everywhere, piles of old papers mounting behind the sofa, stains on the carpet and toys abandoned recklessly on the floor. Moving things aside to find a seat, you switch on the TV and lose yourself while you mindlessly shovel food into your mouth.

If this is how you live at home (or a variation of it), you may take some comfort in it and simply add more and more to the mess. But even if this is not quite how *you* live, let's say you visit someone's home and it's just like this, you may well be tempted to dump your own plate or coffee cup on the already over-piled coffee table. It just fits right in, doesn't it? It's easier to match an environment as you find it than to consider taking your dishes to the kitchen and washing them. We all laugh in the movies when we see someone who is heartbroken and how, a week or two later, a faithful friend comes over to shift them out of the filth and mess. Their environment matches their heartbreak. So, how does your space reflect your inner world …?

In your office, just one crumpled piece of paper thrown carelessly on the floor will demand friends! When clutter is created, it has only one directive issued to it: *Bring friends with you!*

Or how about your bedroom? The bed is unmade, the curtains drawn, dirty laundry lays mixed with clean clothes, make-up, socks, tissues and magazines – just mayhem and chaos. Your briefcase gets slung anywhere, shoes pile up and, as you undress, you simply fling your clothes on the floor to join the others. One more jersey on an already messy pile doesn't make too much difference.

The urbandictionary.com defines the following all-too-familiar *floordrobe* as 'a form of storage for clothing which requires no hangers, drawers, doors or effort. Simply drop on the floor and you have a floordrobe'.

● ●

Whether clutter just seemed to sneak up on you unsuspectingly, or has been lurking in your life in varying degrees ever since you can remember, you need to be warned that it is insidious.

Clutter will take on a life force of its own if you let it. That one little messy corner in your room becomes two, then becomes the whole floor. A mildly untidy area becomes a space you loathe and is eventually a littered office with 10 years of unattended paperwork.

Your medicine cabinet becomes a veritable pharmacy of medicines and toiletries that have long since expired or gone rancid. Your slightly messy living room or den becomes a nightmare TV makeover show in the making. Your kids' bedrooms become a minefield to navigate as everyone tiptoes through the space ignoring it.

As for your body clutter, if you do not detox regularly and take stock of your body's health and wellbeing, you will eventually feel tired, ill, and suffer the consequences of your body telling you, 'Enough is enough!' Isn't it time to keep your body free from clutter and be bouncing with energy?

And lastly, the emotional clutter you carry around and from which you have not allowed yourself to heal, complete things, update your life, move on and process the negative emotions, will fill those glass bottles we talked about earlier with poisonous, sticky, dark goo and create a suit of armor. How heavy is that going to be and how many of your dreams and goals will you have to let slip through your fingers in the process?

If you do not control your clutter, it will control you.

My aim is, firstly, to inspire you and, secondly, to equip you with the right tools to *let go at last*, so you can *live light, live large* and get on with your beautiful life.

Are you ready?

> I was introduced to Kate Emmerson by a mutual friend who lives in London. On meeting Kate and getting to know her better, she urged me to pay attention to some of the aspects in my life that were blocking me from the things I wanted. I was very good at putting myself down, and my self-esteem had taken a knock after the loss of my first business. I had suffered a vicious car-hijacking experience that left me feeling angry, hurt and in fear, and gaining a formidable amount of weight. I believed I was not the same vital, successful person any more and I began to hoard my life with stuff to compensate for the losses I had incurred. Kate began to show me and explain to me that I was not a victim as much as a survivor, and that in the moment I threw myself from the moving car to escape my hijackers I had instead taken a leap of faith and taken control of my circumstances, rather than allowed them to just 'happen to me'.
>
> Slowly I started opening myself up to the idea that my misery was now self-inflicted and that I was now hijacking my own life and preventing myself from growing and moving forward. Kate offered to do a Life Cycle strategy with me ... and it was like a time bomb went off inside of my head. I realized what needed to happen, I immediately started taking charge of my weight and my clutter, I cleared a

garage of old business documents and papers and among them found a retirement annuity policy almost ready to expire, which would ensure a brighter future later down the line. The timing was spot on and everything worked together to turn things around the moment I took that step in the right direction. I have lost half of my weight and am feeling healthier and more vital again every day. As a Christian, too, I believe a lot of what Kate was teaching or unlocking again was about basic universal laws that govern us. Laws that allow us to tap into our vitality and success in this life and call in to being what we desire for ourselves.

Thank you, Kate, for showing and equipping me with the tools I needed to turn my life on again and how to make space for the good stuff. God bless you for your friendship and passion in what you do. xx

Kind regards,
Craig K. Whitehead
Managing Member & Principal Designer: Niche Lifestyle Design cc.

Facing your clutter demons

'We must be willing to let go of the life we have planned, so as to accept the life that is waiting for us.' – Joseph Campbell

Before we can make any real progress, you need to take stock about where you are at the moment. Take a few minutes to complete the clutter assessment checklist as honestly as possible. This is your starting point, and will give you a clear indication of where you are at so you can then decide where you wish to be.

If you always seem to let yourself off the hook when it comes to being brutally honest, perhaps sit with your partner, friend or anyone with whom you feel safe and who is also able to shine a light on this challenging aspect of your life. So often we are blinded out of fear, habit or stress as to the way we are living. We become so used to how we go about each day that we are not able to assess it impartially. Another person can support you and encourage you to be more honest and thus gain the best outcome from this process.

Answer each statement where 1 is the worst you can imagine (clutter/mess) and 10 is the best you can imagine (organized/ordered). To calculate a total for each section, add the values marked in the various columns.

1. PHYSICAL CLUTTER	1	2	3	4	5	6	7	8	9	10
My home is just not organised properly										
My cupboards are a mess or too full										
I have too many clothes I don't wear										
I never throw old things away										
My bedside table is a mess										
I feel physically crowded										
I don't have enough space										
My desk is messy and disorganised										
There are loose papers lying around										
I don't have organised systems										
I have loads of unused magazines, books or CDs										
I get embarrassed if friends visit without warning										
I waste time looking for things										
I have a big area with all sorts of 'junk' in it										
This section's score is										

2. BODY CLUTTER	1	2	3	4	5	6	7	8	9	10
I have been sick more than a couple of days this year										
I get regular headaches, aches and pains										
I have a habit (e.g. smoking) that irritates me										
I wake up feeling tired										
I am agitated and sleep badly most nights										
I suffer from digestion disorders										
I feel lethargic and resort to passive activities such as watching TV										
I battle to focus as much as I would like										
I never take time out to really rejuvenate										
I am always tired at the end of the day										
I exercise less than three times per week										
I drink more than three cups of coffee daily										
I drink more than moderately, which is one drink per day for women and two drinks per day for men										
I eat junk food at least twice a week										
This section's score is										

3. EMOTIONAL CLUTTER	1	2	3	4	5	6	7	8	9	10
I tend to be negative about life or people										
My overdue debt worries me										
I have unfinished relationships that just seem to drag on										
I don't feel connected to the friends I don't see often										
I am very bad at responding to e-mails										
I have overdue or outstanding tax returns										
My finances are in a 'mess' at some level										
I have no motivation or direction in life										
I tend to run late for both business or social engagements										
I am dealing with lots of 'loose ends' that tend to rob me of my energy										
Obligations irritate and drain me										
I have unresolved 'issues' in many areas of my life										
I make commitments but do not fulfil them										
I take things personally and get upset										
This section's score is										
Total score										

If your total score falls between 315 – 420, you'll love learning how to tweak and improve upon existing systems as you already have a sense of order and clarity.

If your total score falls between 189 – 314 you'll be taken on an awesome journey to a clutter free, organized, light life of freedom.

If your total score falls between 0 – 188 then my step-by-step system will help you make inroads never before possible, and you will be amazed at how quickly you can sort your life out with the right support. As we move into the practical steps outlined in Chapter 8, you will be facing all these challenges head on.

How does clutter really affect you?

This section combines all three categories of clutter – physical, body and emotional – and highlights the negative ramifications of holding onto things that no longer serve you.

Precious time

You waste time every day looking for misplaced things, shuffling piles of paper, running late or worrying about unfinished business, while that 'To do' list lurks in the background screaming at you.

You will also be disrespecting time by never being 100% present in whatever you are doing. Your brain and body are so crammed full that there is little left for anything else. Even though you are physically *at* work, you are non-productive, and do everything slowly with no enthusiasm because you feel weighed down or are perhaps hurting deeply about emotional issues so that you are never *present*. You stress about all the stuff you have to do when you get home – and yet, when you get home, you start stressing about all the work you need to do at the office, or the factory, or school. Know that you are doing your spirit a disservice by never being present.

If your *va-va-voom* has up and left, take a moment to think about the time you waste every day by having no systems in place for shopping, housework, chores or effectively handling your e-mail inbox and phone calls. Clutter in all forms robs you of this most precious commodity: Time.

> **FACT:** Getting rid of excess clutter would eliminate 40% of the housework in the average home. – *National Soap and Detergent Association*

Hard-earned money

There is a very real and direct cost in having too much stuff. At the most basic level, consider the money you have spent acquiring what you now own. Then you have to allocate funds to keep it all clean (either doing it yourself or paying someone to do it for you); now add the costly insurance of goods, the cost of storing it all (either in your home or, quite commonly, at off-site storage facilities) and then the high costs of transporting it all when relocating. Some people even have to move into bigger and more expensive homes just to accommodate their stuff.

Clutterers commonly buy triplicates of food, toiletries and clothing simply because they have no idea of what they already have. And even if they know they have it, they have no idea where it is buried or stuffed. You buy yet *another* black shirt, more sneakers, an extra jar of jelly to join the four half-filled containers already in the refrigerator, and another stick of deodorant. It is often easier to buy another than to look for an item, isn't it?

Every single time I clear out clients' homes, I grin when I hear, 'Wow! Now that they're all together I never knew how many tools I had!' Think Tupperware, black shirts, night creams, flashlights, bottle openers … You get the point? The truth is that if you live with clutter, one of the biggest problems is not necessarily the amount of stuff, but how inappropriately it is organized and stored.

Emotional clutter also revolves around not being up to date, being disorganized about life in general, not facing matters head on and dealing with them, for example. Think about the real cost of poor financial habits – high interest accrued by paying bills late, losing bills, not invoicing clients on time, fines or additional penalties from late tax submissions every year.

You will also find hidden money tied up in your neglected belongings or stuff you never use: excessive clothes, books, CDs, exercise equipment, furniture and ornaments. When clients bleat that they cannot afford to pay for professional clutter-clearing services, I remind them that 80% of my clients recoup up to a third of the fee by off-loading their clutter.

Two out of every three clients I see are devaluing one of their most expensive possessions by not being able to park their cars in the garage because the garage is stuffed full!

It is also common, every time you clear up, to find money, both literally or figuratively. People find change and notes in the weirdest places, checks that have never been cashed, receipts that help them claim on tax expenses or missing policies worth money. Remember Craig on page 33?

People who lug around excess emotional or mental clutter and do not live a clear, light-hearted life will try to fill an emotional hole by shopping, wasting time or gathering things around them to feel momentarily uplifted and loved. What they end up doing, however, is spending money instead of spending positive energy on fixing up their lives.

Sapped energy

Living with any of the three categories of clutter wastes energy, leaving you feeling dull, lethargic and clogged up in the literal sense of the term and with zero flow of vital energy in your body. Clutter means living in the past and hangs about with its playmate, procrastination. Remember the image of the fishing line with lead weights at the end? You are being pulled down.

Hiding behind your physical clutter could mean that you are hiding from life, playing small, burying emotional pain and getting stuck in your past. Hiding out behind your body issues – illness, pain, excess weight, eating disorders, guzzling over-the-counter medications – often means saying *no* to life or *no* to opportunities by offering a 'valid excuse': I'm too tired; I have a sore back – you know what I mean!

Your attachment to anything that no longer serves you steals your spiritual energy as you become overly attached to material possessions, which you can't even take with you. We have a warped sense of what is important and allow our belongings to chain us rather than to enhance our lives. It's almost as if we refuse to live mindfully in the present and continue to experience that heavy feeling, one that is nebulous to describe yet tangible to our spirit.

The shame, guilt, fear, resentment, chaos and anger that get tangled up with all forms of clutter simply mean you never allow yourself to be the best version of yourself.

Cramped creativity

When you live with clutter, your thinking is clouded; you will have no inspiration and feel so overwhelmed that it becomes impossible to formulate new ideas or creative solutions to your problems.

It is as if you are wearing a blindfold to your life. You cannot see exciting opportunities because all your 'stuff' is blocking the view. Can you remember how fabulous it was the last time you cleared one space, be it your handbag, a drawer, your desk, and how it immediately lifted your spirits?

Imagine the profound effect when your entire life is clear.

Procrastination kills creativity because you are always playing catch-up with yourself, never letting yourself off the hook by being up to date. The longer you leave it, the thicker the blindfold becomes.

Ripped-up reputation

Clutterers tend to be nagged by a feeling of being totally disorganized or unprofessional, and constantly berate themselves. Clutter creates feelings of shame, deep embarrassment and a zero sense of control. There is an energy of 'laziness', as well as being in 'victim mode' when clutter is present.

Not having dealt effectively with past issues, not having enough energy or *vooma* to face your life, worrying about too many issues, having too many tasks incomplete and matters unresolved, leads to regularly not 'showing up'. And when you constantly show up late for life, social events and meetings, miss deadlines, forget facts, never feel in charge and are always flustered and highly stressed, you give off the wrong vibes. The sad truth is that people judge us – whether we like it or not – on what they first see and experience when they meet us. According to Mike Bova, Vice President of M3P Media LLC, statistics show that first impressions are made in the first 20 seconds, and a bad first impression takes up to an additional 20 contacts to rectify and shift that bad first impression.

The bottom line is that if your clutter is impacting your professional or personal life, then your reputation, career and relationships could be at stake.

An eye-opening way to think about it is to imagine people – a prospective boss, a promising new client, a potential lover or new best friend – having the ability to sneak an all-access peek into your life both seen and unseen. In other words, they get an unrestricted view into how you live your life … Now, honestly, would they be dying to meet or hire you, or dying to run a mile?

Your reputation is vital, and your clutter can crush it.

Clutter audit

I'm going to suggest that you now take the clutter assessment checklist one step further, to get a real nuts-and-bolts reality kick. Nothing like the shock factor to awaken your motivation and to inspire you to get sorted.

Step 1: Don't read any further until you have completed this step, okay?

Looking at the assessment you completed earlier, see if you can honestly account for how much time each of the statements are chewing up in your day. In other words, allocate how much time you honestly waste per day.

For example, you may waste five minutes every time you look for your car keys, and you drive approximately six times a day with kids, shopping, work, hobbies and sport commitments. So that adds up to 30 minutes per day.

Work your way down the list to see where you waste time, allocating two minutes here, 10 minutes there. *Mmm* … If you are honest, that argument you play over and over and over in your head every day is, truthfully, taking up 45 minutes; the five-minute snooze every morning after the alarm goes off; the energy slump every afternoon – note it *all*. What about every time you interrupt a task when e-mail beeps into your inbox? Be ruthless!

Grab your calculator and add it all up. Now you have the number of minutes (or even hours) you waste every day. It is estimated that, on average, people waste 50 minutes per day just looking for things.

Keep this tally of minutes or hours aside and now clear your calculator.

Step 2: Key your monthly take-home salary, allowance, pension – in other words, your income – into the calculator.

Step 3: Divide this figure by 176 – the average number of hours worked in a 22-day month, 8 hours a day. Alternatively, you can also work out how much time you realistically work per month, and divide your salary by your more accurate figure if you choose. Whichever method you choose, the fact remains that the figure staring back at you from the calculator screen is the amount you earn per hour.

Step 4: Now multiply the amount you earn per hour (your figure from Step 3) by the total time wasted per day calculated in Step 1.

Step 5: Then multiply this figure by 365 – and chances are you're slapping yourself right now as you begin to understand the amount of money you waste per year through your various forms of clutter!

EXAMPLE
Step 1 – You assess you waste on average 1.5 hours per day.
Step 2 – Your take home salary is 35 000.
Step 3 – 35 000 / 176 (work hours per month) = 198.86 / hour
Step 4 – 198.86 x 1.5 (hours wasted per day) = 298.29 / day
Step 5 – 298.29 x 365 = 108 877.83 / year

108 877.03 is the amount of moolah, cash, bucks, dollars – you name it – wasted every year!

I don't care what currency you're working in, that is a *lot* of money – money that could be put towards education, bond payments, holidays, new business or a professional clutter clearing in your life!

So now that you have been brutally honest, how is your motivation factor? Why not come on over to my Facebook page https://www.facebook.com/kate.emmerson.page right now and tell us how you feel and how much *you* are wasting – if you dare?

The cost of your clutter demon runs deep and wide. Imagine the possibility you could unlock as you use that time, money and energy for more exhilarating pursuits.

Now let's take a look at the psychological aspects that surround your clutter so you really get to understand what is holding you back and why.

6

Why all the invisible fishing lines?

Before you can really get stuck into doing the step-by-step process of clutter clearing, we need to spend more time unpacking the reasons as well as the excuses behind the clutter. This is the *why*. *Why* did it all get started in the first place? In other words, what was your turning point?

You need to uncover the root cause that allowed you to attach all those fishing lines to your solar plexus so that, as you become aware of it, you can start to heal and then allow yourself to work with all those root-cause lines rather than against them.

You need to cut all those fishing lines and bottles filled with lead in order to *live light, live large*.

What is really going on?

Set aside some quiet time to respond – off the top of your head – to the following questions. Don't read through them all yet. Simply start at the top and be *honest*. You might find you need to come back to certain questions again and again. Bear in mind all three categories of clutter: physical, body and emotional. Your clutter may offer insights if you just take some time to understand it and let it 'dialogue' with you.

Here goes …

1. After realizing how much time and money I waste on clutter, I …
2. Clutter is generally …
3. The worst thing about my clutter is …
4. The biggest challenge I have with my clutter is …
5. If other people knew how I lived my life – emotionally, physiologically and physically in my space – they might …
6. If I was to suddenly die today, what state would I leave my 'affairs' in and how much would someone have to 'clean up' after me?
7. That reality of my death makes me feel …
8. If I named my clutter challenge in its entirety, as if it was the title of a book, mine would be …
9. What does my clutter represent to me?
10. How does my clutter serve me? (This can be a tough one to answer because clutterers will vehemently state it doesn't serve them in any way and they would sort it out if only they had the time or energy. But, in some way, it *is* anchoring you in that state of 'stuckness', that state of fear in which you are choosing to live. Having the clutter is keeping you 'safe' somehow.) So, once again, How does my clutter serve me?
11. If I look back, I can remember my clutter situation started …
12. I was feeling _____ at that time.
13. What else was happening at that time?
14. Who else was involved?
15. What would I be doing if I didn't have clutter in my life?
16. Why am I so scared of that possibility?
17. I battle to take responsibility for …
18. I feel most out of control when …
19. I feel totally overwhelmed in the face of …
20. I want to run away when …
21. Whenever I have tried to clear clutter before, I usually …

Phew, that's probably given you a few things to ponder … Now read Lisa's story on the opposite page as she shares her compelling understanding of why she had been living with so much clutter all her life. While she keeps saying she did not complete the course, her transformation seems to jump off the page – let her inspire *you!*

Dear Kate,

I did not do the complete de-clutter course, simply because it's hard work and requires commitment to change, but there was also additional factors, like the fact that I, my hubby and both our sons are ADD and our lives are chaotic. I also have chronic pain, depression, am scarred from losing five babies and having had a physically abusive childhood till the age of 19 when I choked my mother who abused me – she never ever hit me again.

I grew up being also materially deprived – my mother bought lots of clothes for herself and I had to wear her cast-offs, once we were the same size – imagine a 16-year-old wearing her mother's old clothes and the other girls knowing it – my self-esteem was virtually non-existent though I hid that fact quite well.

My childhood predisposed me to being a pack rat. [It] was and still is difficult for me not to hoard stuff: mismatched socks can still be worn to keep your feet warm, old T-shirts whose color has faded can be dyed again – just to mention a few of my rationalizations to hold on to stuff. [With] the socks it was [simply] the memory of cold, wet feet in winter especially [that] was so deeply entrenched that without conscious thought I was holding onto stuff in my 'deprived mode'.

Books and papers were kept because the info/knowledge are useful and I loved owning books of my own – though reading over 100 Barbara Cartland paperbacks and storing them under your bed is simply a dust catcher.

I got your de-clutter course via e-mail, I read it every week and started to take stock of my life, at least my clutter.

I was sitting with bags of clothes, crates and boxes of books and papers which, in lots of cases, I had forgotten what was contained therein.

I started sorting things out and giving away what is useful for others. I joined the Cape Town Freecycle group, but despite it all it was not easygoing. [My] rate of clutter and [accumulation] was still more than me sorting things out.

I now sort out my stuff once a quarter and there is less clutter. I have a rudimentary storing system for my hobby stuff, where there used to be none.

Reading those e-mails from u took root more strongly than I knew. The de-clutter course drew a direct correlation between the chaos of the internal and the external environment and how it can and in some cases does impact on the mental wellbeing – the worse thing for someone who suffers from depression is to live in a cluttered chaotic environment.

The de-clutter course forced me to face up to why I am a packrat and through that process I was able to consciously accept that my material conditions have changed and therefore I could and should too.

It's been over two years and in that period I have gotten rid of broken furniture that I never got around to fixing, as well as papers, books and clothes. [My] home is not how I want it to be yet but it is less untidy, less cluttered and seems bigger and therefore easier to clean.

If I implemented the de-clutter [program] completely I would no doubt have progressed more, but the few sections of the course/program I was exposed to had a life-changing effect and impact on me – my marriage is better for it – my husband and I quarreled a lot about my packrat habits – that is a thing of the past. ADD people need uncluttered, structured environments to function optimally – I am on my way to it.

Your course/program helped me to have a couple of mind shifts/changes from which I benefit up till today, because the [program] focuses on both a person's material environment as well as teaches one to ask critical questions of oneself as to why we are the way we are, do things the way we do and where [it started]. It forces one [into] a position to face weak, disorganized areas and strengthens them. The impact ... lasts way beyond the duration of the program and, as a self-help junkie, the only program of its kind that deals with a 'simple' issue of clutter but ultimately leads to an improvement of one's external and internal environment – the skills learned through the program have become part of my skill set and impacts until today.

Kate, I hate typing, but it is only fair that I say thank you and that, while I did not complete the program, it has a continuing and profound impact and effect on my life and the home I created for my family.

Thank you.

Sincerely,
Lisa McBride

Excuses, excuses, excuses

The truth is we are all capable of clearing up our lives if we truly want to. Yet we allow ourselves to be overwhelmed by the enormity of the task – so much so that it becomes too much to even consider. What stops us is the myriad excuses we make, the masks we hide behind and the lies we tell ourselves. We let ourselves off the hook by replaying all sorts of excuses – excuses that hold us back, keep us stuck where we are, allowing our self-limiting beliefs to run our lives.

See if you recognize yourself in some of the following excuses, compiled from thousands of clients over the years.

- 'I have clutter because I inherited it from my Gran.'
- 'My friends went overseas and left their stuff with me – five years ago.'
- 'I couldn't clear it when my mother died and here it still is …'
- 'I moved into a smaller place and just can't get organized.'
- 'I've been too busy since my kids were born.' (The youngest is now six!)
- 'I work full time and I am a single parent – I'm not superhuman, you know.'
- 'I lost my confidence when I was fired and don't know how to get started.'
- 'I work from home and don't have enough space.'
- 'I don't know how to stop shopping!'
- 'I'm addicted to [bargains/sales/discount coupons].'
- 'My weight fluctuates, so I need thin *and* fat clothes.'
- 'Only people as bad as those on the TV makeover shows really have a problem.'
- 'I love trinkets, treasures and antiques – they make me happy.'
- 'I don't have clutter; I just collect things …'
- 'I just don't have enough time and money to sort it out.'
- 'I'm too tired after work and don't know where to start.'
- 'What's the point? It'll just get bad again …'
- 'What if I need it when it's gone?'
- 'I've got too much on my mind to bother clearing clutter now.'
- 'I'll never put things back so it's useless even trying.'
- 'I can't think straight so I'll never be able to tackle clutter.'
- 'They were wrong, so why should I forgive them?'
- 'How can I have a tidy house with three kids and no housekeeper?'
- 'People gave me this stuff so I suppose I have to keep it …'
- 'I paid good money for this!'
- 'I'll fit into it one day so I can't get rid of it.'

- 'I hate wasting stuff and throwing it away.'
- 'I like all my stuff and it cost me money.'
- 'I hated being told to tidy up as a kid.'
- 'If you don't have things in your home, then you're emotionally cold.'
- 'I have never been good with systems and always lose things.'
- 'All creative people are messy and live in chaos.'
- 'My environment has nothing to do with my feelings.'
- 'I have always been overweight.'
- 'I was a sickly child and I still battle to take control of my health.'
- 'I have no energy to tackle it.'
- 'I've been sick three times this year and just can't get started.'
- 'Everyone lives on pills and junk food to cope, don't they?'
- 'I love food too much to lose weight.'
- 'I'm not tired – I just do too much at work.'
- 'It's normal to have headaches and feel tired every day, isn't it?'
- 'I really have gotten over him/her – I'm just not into meeting anyone else.'
- 'My partner messes up what I keep tidy.'
- 'They are so lazy; it's not me!'
- 'I am so worried about my finances that I feel like a deer in headlights.'
- 'I am very stressed and unhappy and have no motivation.'
- 'I think I might be depressed because I cry every day.'
- 'I get angry in the traffic every day – at least five times a day!'
- 'My life feels like it's going nowhere …'
- 'I'll never meet someone. Who will ever fall in love with me?'
- 'I'm so useless and am not making anything of myself.'
- 'I have never cared about my appearance or my wardrobe.'
- 'I'm always late, just like my dad was …'
- 'I've always been disorganized and pay my bills late.'
- 'We fight over the house all the time – why does it matter?'

As you read Noni's story, which follows, you may understand that she too could have made up any number of excuses – you will see snippets of Noni throughout this book.

> 2010 was one heck of a year for me, a real life-changing experience! After separating [from] my husband [after] six years in 2009, we decided to legalize the divorce. I moved out (with my little brother, whom I've always been a guardian to). Shortly after that, in February 2010, my sister passed away, which meant I had to now be a legal guardian to her then 12-year-old daughter as well. I don't do pity

parties very well, so I decided to do what had to be done. I thought, You know what, life has presented me with the challenges of being married at 19 years old, divorced at 25 and being a parent to two teenagers overnight (in addition to my profession). With a sore heart and daily tears, I found an apartment, school, transport to school for the kids and I obviously could [not] afford a full-time helper so that was not an option. 2010 was my year of going to work with puffy eyes, kids' homework, sport, smiling when I didn't want to, but we all made it through, surprisingly the kids with very impressive year-end reports too!

The kids and I decided that boarding school was the best option. They are happily off to Vaal Christian Boarding School. I have an opportunity to be a normal 26-year-old. I know there is so [much] I can offer. I am ready to rebuild my life, explore who Nonelela is (not as wife, sister, aunt, but as **me**). This could not have come at a better time!

[The] single most important aspect I'd like to change with Kate's help is the financial aspect. I did not get anything from my marriage. I literally had clothes and the car to my name **only**. I started from scratch and have incurred some debt and have been heavily burdened with all the responsibilities.

Just 18 months later, in 2012, Noni wrote the following:

Oh my gosh! I have just gone through everything from your course ... It's amazing how far I've come! If I were you, Kate, I'd be so proud of myself for the work I am doing in people's lives.

Do you realize just how impactful you have been in my life? How you have changed my life through your work?

Thank you so much, Kate! I have paid up my car in full and bought a house. I have also taken up an investment policy. I do have some debt but am not over-debted at all.

*The principles I acquired through your **Spring clean your life** (to clear my clutter) and **Ignite your life** (to get back on track) programs did wonders as some of my 'potatoes' were debt related.*

I am in a very healthy, great relationship. We have a seven-month-old son born on 24 January 2012 ... and I have now been promoted to Divisional Training Manager.

Nonelela Xaba (Noni)
Division Training Manager 2012, SPAR South Rand

The energy underlying clutter

Want to know the five real reasons we get caught up with clutter? Then read on ...

1. Guilt

We keep many things out of obligation to someone else, usually dead!

One of the most significant factors that keep people stuck with clutter is the overwhelming sense of guilt because of the attachment we have to where and who it came from. Not only do we inherit patterns of behaviors from our family or caregivers, but often when they die we also inherit their 'stuff' – whether we want it or not. I am often called in to assist families when a loved one has passed on, because they either cannot bear to confront the emotional turmoil, or they know that if they clear it out themselves they will simply keep it all.

People feel a responsibility to be good stewards of things, says Randy Frost, professor of Psychology at Smith College, in Northampton, Massachusetts, and a co-author of *Buried in Treasures* (Oxford University Press, 2007). This is especially true of items they've been given by or inherited from a loved one. Getting rid of a present feels like disrespecting the giver. But we tend to forget the true meaning of gifts in the first place.

Are you being suffocated by stuff inherited from your family? Have you even stopped noticing it's there? I know that the thought of getting rid of it, passing it on or selling it makes you question your loyalty and ask, 'Am I a bad person because I don't want this item even though it was Granny's?' Or do you lament over the fact that you *have* to keep these because they were your mother's *favorite* tablecloths – all 43 of them!

When you keep 'stuff' out of guilt, you are in effect giving other people control over your life. Your challenge is to realize that items do not equal the person or the memory of that person. Life is not about accumulating stuff – it is about the experience of being. If someone else's possessions are trapping you out of guilt, it's time to look within and ask yourself some tough questions. Find new and more creative ways to hold onto the memories of a loved one – perhaps one tea set can be representative of Gran, rather than every single thing she owned. As callous as it seems, the deceased person doesn't actually care, so every time you hear their voice in your head, it's all your own doing!

Just this week I met someone at one of my talks who has all her deceased grandmother's stuff in her garage, and she squealed that she is not 'allowed' to get rid of it because her mother is attached to it. My answer: 'Then give it back to your mother if she wants her mother's stuff, and get Granny's stuff out of *your* garage.'

Let's also talk about unwanted gifts! Do you have cupboards full of gifts you don't love, don't match your personality or home and yet you're paralyzed at the thought of passing them on? Remember the old adage that it's the *thought* behind the gift that counts – *that* is what's more important. Create your own gift cupboard, where you can go 'shopping' whenever you need to – just be careful that if you're going to recycle gifts, then remember who gave you what so you don't land up in hot water.

And what about the topic of sentimental cards, letters, children's art creations, baby teeth and the like? How on earth can we part with stuff that has such meaning? I am a bad person if I throw away anything that was made out of love or relates to my child's development. What kind of a monster am I to not keep it all? The trick is to keep just a few items that represent the whole. Not every single thing.

If you happen to live in a home that can comfortably accommodate 50 people, well then … sure, you could keep all you want, but the rule of thumb would still stand: Ensure that it *serves* you, and serves you *now*!

Keeping anything out of guilt just feeds that negative emotion, and nothing done from a place of guilt is ever truly aligned to who you are.

2. Fear

Fear indicates a lack of trust in the 'universe'.

One of the most common responses to my question, 'Why can't you let this go?' is: 'What if I need it one day? Let me keep it just in case.' If this is your stock response, you will probably also have many, many stories to support your belief:

- 'Well, once when I let go of my red cocktail dress, I got invited to a party that week and I needed it.'
- 'When I threw out the magazines, I remembered the important article I had meant to cut out.'
- 'I always need it just after I throw it out.'

Yes, we can find examples to support our deepest fears and excuses all the time but now it's time to challenge them. These examples serve to highlight how we con ourselves into keeping everything. We say we need the magazines for recipes or information on some travel destination, yet continue to pile them up in the corner without another glance and we work so hard we don't ever make time to take that long-awaited trip.

What about flow, energy, movement? Just as our bodies are homeostatic systems that always strive to regulate themselves, so our lives should reflect that. Remember when we discussed nature and how it needs to flow – how awesome to apply that rule to your inner and external life.

Living with this kind of fear indicates a complete lack of trust in the universe. As I write this chapter, I am sitting in the bush near the Botswana border – what a beautiful office I've created – and this morning on a game drive I was contemplating how obvious nature is. It simply exists, in the moment. While each animal or plant species might have its unique, inherent way of storing water or food, the predominant aspect of nature is to wake up at first light every day, and simply respond to the day as it unfolds. They go looking for food and shelter and simply exist. We get such a sense of calm, peace and fulfillment when we witness nature at its best. When last were you at the sea, in the bush, on top of a mountain or deep in a forest to absorb the magnificence of nature?

We would do well to apply that to our own lives. I am not talking about living like an ascetic or the life of a monk, but to simply question the excess to which we have become accustomed. While I am the first to admit to loving beautiful things, do we really need 10 crystal decanters, 20 sets of linen and

50 rolls of crumpled wrapping paper along with 200 old cassette tapes we can no longer even listen to?

Heed the call to revert to simplicity, having absolutely everything that you need and want, without having stuff for all the wrong reasons.

We wake up every morning and usually trust that we have enough air to breathe – we don't try to gulp all the air we need for our waking hours. We subconsciously trust that it will always be there. And we *b-r-e-a-t-h-e*.

Imagine being able to shed all the fear associated with your 'stuff' and being able to live with a deeper connection to the universe, a sense of lightness, and a belief that if you do get rid of all that no longer serves you, for whatever reason, you will be able to replace it when necessary. Yes, even your fat/thin clothes – you will be able to replace them with something more appropriate and gorgeous when you want to.

There is another association with fear – and that is the modern idea that somehow more is better. It proves our success, status and standing when we are able to 'show off' in the world as opposed to 'show up'. We make ourselves feel better by filling the void with possessions – so even if we might be hiding what's really going on inside (the facade's okay but the interior is crumbling), we have a false sense of acceptance from the outside world when we keep up with the Joneses.

In effect, we run from the fear of 'what if people find out that we are not okay, things are not happy in the home, I've just lost my job, my kid is bulimic, I take drugs, we're drowning in debt?' We fear showing our true selves to the world, so holding onto things and gathering more and more around ourselves, do a wonderful job of feeding that fear. If your stuff is suffocating you and making you distrust the universe, or you are hiding out from the world behind your facade, it's time to drop that storyline.

Fear is also the reason why we use 'stuff' to suppress our negative emotions. Fear is false, always covering up other emotions bubbling just beneath the surface: feelings of not being good enough, anger, resentment, betrayal, loss, failure, lack of self-worth and so on. If we are not able to naturally process the hurt and pain that fuels our fear, we will trip ourselves up. We might first fill internal spaces and start to mistreat our bodies at a physiological level by eating and drinking the wrong things, contributing to excess weight, illness, toxins and lethargy. Then we might also fill our external spaces with stuff so that we are literally filling up the holes inside of ourselves – and leaving no room to think or feel.

Your external environment therefore simply reflects what is going on emotionally, spiritually and mentally. And clutter fills the empty spaces, becoming the very reason that you do not have to address your life, your hurts, and your pain. What are you avoiding? Because whatever it is, it is all being stored in your clutter – but at what cost to you and your life? Just like holding a big beach ball under water, it really takes more energy to keep your emotions suppressed.

3. Scarcity

Scarcity indicates lack of abundance.

Another reason a lot of people hoard stuff is because they have a scarcity mentality. We have spent our hard-earned money on something so we feel obliged to squeeze every last drop out of it, no matter what – even if we no longer like it (or never did).

This mindset can also stem from having grown up in a state of deprivation – be it as a result of war, depression, famine, the Holocaust, refugee status or due to death of family at a young age. As a result, you are left with the scars of having had nothing, or having had everything taken from you. Rather than facing the battle of working on healing those deep wounds to give you freedom today, you might choose – subconsciously even – to remain stuck in the pattern of scarcity and hold on for dear life.

Because you are, understandably, not able to grasp the idea that as you let go you make space for new to flow in, you work from the premise that you have to keep everything simply for the sake of keeping, because one day it may all be taken away. If you have grown up with no food, no freedom, no new clothes, no family, no peace, no warm bed, no choice, it is not difficult to understand how this can create habits of holding on, or in extreme cases, hoarding. It shows up as excess in every way: a sense of desperation about owning things, eating too much food at the buffet because it is there, taking every free gift and sale item home with you rather than leaving it on the shelf. A scarcity mentality will always take the little bottles of shampoo and hand cream from the hotel, and will be drawn to coupon shopping.

If this is your story, and you have managed to make a huge success of your life, you may also be one of those A-type personalities who have to have a hundred of everything, from cars to ties, shoes to bags, businesses to parties to holidays. You revel in excess simply because you can. Your ego can become attached to things you own and, rather than remembering what really matters, your life revolves around how much you have and how much control you have over it, including people.

It does not matter how you choose to live or spend your money; all that matters is that you live your real, authentic life – and are not hiding out behind your stuff. That's all.

4. Insecurity

I have, therefore I exist.

I often hear clients tell stories of how the things they keep give them a sense of belonging, a sense of past, a sense of achievement and a sense of identity. Accumulating collections of things – whiskey, stamps, cards, pub memorabilia, ticket stubs, paper money from countries visited, baseball caps, photos, you name it – can be a reassurance that you *exist*.

One of my clients, Joy, had 12 years' worth of movie ticket stubs – every one she had ever been to with her husband. When I felt them in the back of the cupboard I thought I had struck oodles of cash, and we shrieked with laughter as we realized what they were. It had been years since she had even looked at them, yet there they were taking up precious space in a room that was unlivable. In the end, she was able to keep just **one** movie stub (in front of a live studio audience on *Let's chat with Mel*, M-Net) as a memento of her life, and beautify it with her incredible scrapbooking talent. She thus allowed 'one' to represent the 'many'.

That stuffed room was transformed on camera into an office/scrapbooking space in just five hours and very soon became a nursery for her first baby! She shared with me how easy it was, after it was cleared, to accept new blessings into their lives.

Your school reports, for example, serve to prove you existed, and even excelled at something. The trophies you won, the first course you completed at work, your first contract of employment are all external proof of the hours you spent studying, learning, living, competing. But all these external items are simply your attempt to validate who you are. It can be useful to keep the most precious ones, the ones that hold the most powerful positive energy for you, such as your favorite letters (but not every single one). As you start believing in your real sense of self, the less is your *need* to have stuff around you. It becomes about mindful choice. Security can never come from belongings; in fact, the opposite is often true because the more stuff you have the more you worry about it being taken from you.

5. Hoarding

The extreme cases …

Here is some information to help you understand the growing phenomenon that is hoarding. Most people think that extreme hoarders are simply lazy slobs, but that is far from the case. This is a condition in which holding on becomes an obsession and letting go elicits paralyzing fear.

Dr Julie Pike, a psychologist at the Anxiety Disorders Treatment Center in Durham, North Carolina, says of hoarding: 'It's a debilitating condition where [hoarders] accumulate clutter to the point of impairment. We estimate two million people in the U.S. have this problem, but we can't be exactly sure because people who hoard are very secretive about it.'

The Mayo Clinic (www.mayoclinic.com) says the following: 'Hoarding is the excessive collection of items, along with the inability to discard them. Hoarding often creates such cramped living conditions that homes may be filled to capacity, with only narrow pathways winding through stacks of clutter. Some people also collect animals, keeping dozens or hundreds of pets often in unsanitary conditions.'

Now that you may have seen yourself in some of the reasons for clutter, it comes down to the nitty-gritty: What are we going to *do* about it? While all the theory is a vital first step to understanding, it needs to be backed up with action that will lead to transformation. *Your* transformation.

Creating space and moving forward

'Everything should be made as simple as possible, but not simpler.'
– Albert Einstein

I – the Quick Shift Deva – promise you that this process will change your life by giving you energy, space and order, like it has for the thousands who have completed this step-by-step process. One day at a time.

The power of clutter clearing never ceases to amaze me, and every time I hear stories from clients or work with someone in their home and see the transformation before my eyes, it reaffirms the incredible power of letting go! I will keep sharing clients' testimonials to inspire you and keep you moving forward so you too can come to the realization that, just as others have managed to get through it, you can too!

I know you're willing to jump in and sort out your clutter, but I also understand that the sheer weight, volume and magnitude of the huge task at hand has up until now stopped you dead in your tracks. My gift is to be able to guide you gently through the process without letting you off the hook, so you can finally feel the joy of sorting out your clutter.

Join the online community

When you feel a little low and are wondering how to carry on with your clutter and everything I throw your way each day, tap into the collective energy of others walking the same journey with you! That is why I have created a unique online platform where you can read others' stories, post your own insights and connect with others.

E-mail marketing@kate-emmerson.com and request the invite – see you online!

Commitment

Right ... Are you ready to commit to shifting the clutter in your life?

My intention is to nudge (sometimes prod!) and point you in the right direction every day so that you spend focused time working through all the cluttered areas of your life. I will share some knowledge with you regarding the topic for the day, and then we will get stuck into actually *doing* it. Ideally, you need to commit an hour every day (be creative and find time to fit it in) in order to get the full benefit of what is outlined here. If you can encourage anyone else you may live with to do it with you, even better, but don't let him or her stop you.

It is important to remember, however, that – depending on your personal clutter circumstances – you may complete the daily task in a slightly shorter time, or you might need to take a couple of days to complete it. I suggest that you do something every day! So the hour timeline is a guideline, and each day could be different for you. The bottom line is that over the next 28 days you will reclaim control of your life, stop making excuses for all the clutter you have accumulated, and simply dedicate *one* hour a day to do whatever I throw your way. Deal?

I cannot force you to clear out your life, and the mere fact that you have read this far, although a good sign, may not be enough when the going gets tough. Come and join the community for additional support so that I can help you in a practical way to stay on track.

Yes, you have still got to get off your behind, literally and figuratively, and do what needs to be done! There is no polite or easy way to say it. We focus on a small area every day, which will facilitate the process and make it much easier for you to wade through your 'stuff'. Before you know it, the weeks will be over and your life will be so much fresher and clearer.

Make each day really count!

If you have a day when it seems impossible to find time (yes, we all have those 'off' days, even with the best of intentions) then simply catch up over the weekend when you can. But make sure your 'off' days are not every other day, because then you're simply conning yourself or making excuses.

Before you continue any further … go and grab yourself a huge glass of water to drink as you continue reading. It can be cold and spruced up with some lemon, or hot and jazzed up with some fresh ginger. Off you go … right now!

This will be an ongoing task – that you drink at least 500 ml of water as you're completing your daily task!

Morning Kate,

Two years ago I decided to de-clutter my life and ended up selling and giving away about 80% of our belongings. I even got 'rid' of my husband and children as they were drowning me. I took a year off and filled my jug and we are all now back together and have never been happier. If I didn't de-clutter my life at that point I would have had a nervous breakdown. My husband and children now appreciate me and I enjoy spending time with them and they no longer take me for granted. I know it was a bit extreme, but it was the best thing I have ever done.

Regards,
Laurel

What do you wish to manifest through your clutter clearing?

This may seem an odd thing to ask, but by this I mean more than the obvious aspects of getting rid of clutter, enjoying more space and being more organized. Those outcomes are a given, provided you stick to the daily tasks. I mentioned earlier that the energy of your clutter stops you from moving forward and keeps you stagnant and stuck. So, as you start clearing it all out and letting go, you will start to make in-roads to something new and exciting waiting just around the corner.

So, what do you truly wish to manifest for yourself? It could be:

- A new job
- An exciting promotion
- Your soul mate
- New clients
- A new home
- A fabulous vacation
- Improved cash flow
- Peace of mind
- A new circle of friends
- A new hobby
- New, positive habits and attitudes
- The successful opening of a new venture
- Spiritual reflection
- Improved self-confidence
- The courage to move forward
- Exciting opportunities

Take a moment now to decide your *reason*, the motivation that is going to keep you going. This will help you stay focused and give you something to strive for when you get stuck, overwhelmed or find it difficult to part with something.

It will be useful to remind yourself of your goal as you work through the program so that you move forward with clarity and direction. By declaring your intention, you will find it easier to let go of the old and make space for the new. So let's harness that energy!

This will be your mantra, your reinforcement every day:

> **Today I am letting go of XYZ, which no longer serve me, in order to make space for _____.**

(Fill in what you wish to manifest, such as 'a promotion at work'.)

You see, whether your clutter relates directly to what you wish to manifest or not, it has the same underlying essence of energy. The aim is to let go of *all* the things that no longer serve you, in all three categories of clutter and to work towards a common goal.

Got it! Lets commit to the practical step-by-step process at last.

Share your story with Kate and get additional support:

1. Pick up phone.
2. Go onto our Facebook page.
3. Like our Facebook page.
4. Share what you wish to manifest through your clearing.

8

Let's do it – day by day

'Whether you're aware of it or not, clutter creates indecision and distractions, consuming attention and making unfettered happiness a real chore.' – Timothy Ferriss, author of *The 4-hour Work Week*

Day 1 - Preparation guidelines

I bet you have several questions before we begin, so read through the following guidelines and get a head start on the practicalities of the overall process. We'll dive into the real *doing* tomorrow. Planning ahead is important.

Water

This is *the* most important ingredient you can be putting in your body on a daily basis, and for the next 28 days *and beyond*, it is vital that you get into this habit if you have not already. You need to be drinking at least 6-8 glasses of water a day! This does not include the water in tea or coffee, which actually dehydrates rather than replenish. I suggest that you keep a bottle of spring water with you at all times.

If you do not relish the thought of just water, then add a drop of fruit juice, fresh lemon, herbal tea or mint, for example, to make it more appealing. Water clears your body of toxins and other bodily clutter, by mobilizing the blood, the lymphatic system and kidneys, which all help to filter our bodies. It will also give your more energy – dehydration causes sluggishness.

For more on the healing powers of water, read the fascinating work of Fereydoon Batmanghelidj MD at www.watercure.com. Dr Batmanghelidj, an internationally renowned researcher, author and advocate of the natural healing power of water, was born in Iran in 1931. When the Iranian Revolution broke out in 1979, he was placed in the infamous Evin Prison as a political prisoner for two years and seven months. It was there that he discovered the healing powers of water. One night, Dr B had to treat a fellow prisoner with crippling peptic ulcer pain. With no medications at his disposal, Dr B gave him two glasses of water. Within eight minutes, the man's pain disappeared. He was instructed to drink two glasses of water every three hours and became absolutely pain free for his four remaining months in the prison. Dr B successfully treated 3 000 fellow prisoners suffering from stress-induced peptic ulcer disease with water alone. Dr Batmanghelidj wrote his first self-help book, *Your Body's Many Cries for Water* in 1992, in which he stated that a dry mouth is not a reliable indicator of dehydration. The body signals its water shortage by producing pain. Dehydration actually produces pain and many degenerative diseases, including asthma, arthritis, hypertension, angina, adult-onset diabetes, lupus and multiple sclerosis. Dr B's message to the world is, 'You are not sick, you are thirsty. Don't treat thirst with medication.'

'When Dr Batmanghelidj thinks of a glass of water, he doesn't think of it as half full or half empty. He thinks of it as brimming over with the essential fluid of life. He thinks of it as the solvent of our ills and deliverer of ripe old age. He thinks of it as the wave of the future.' – *The Washington Times*

Other people's clutter

Quite simply, it is *not* your place to work with other people's clutter. If you cohabit with others, you need to be mindful that *you* have chosen to do this, not them, unless they've agreed to the process with you. You will probably find that as you start clearing out your clutter, they may be inspired to do the same. If you have small kids under the age of 10, you can absolutely enlist their help. In fact they usually find it much easier to let go of things, and can thus teach us about the real meaning of spring-cleaning.

If you have teenagers, leave their rooms well alone! If their clutter is lying in the common areas of the house, you can ask them to remove it to their personal space, but thereafter it is in their territory. So, although it may be tough, make sure that you deal with your stuff only. In this case, it's all about *you*!

When you get to shared possessions or spaces, rather enlist your partner's help and support, and you can decide what to do together. You will need to be very tactful and mindful, because we can get very attached to our clutter, and if you simply go ahead and throw other people's stuff out, you deny them the process of cleansing and clearing out for themselves.

Bring on the boxes

Have the following with you every time, as they will make your life so much easier. You will need five boxes or large trash bags, whichever you prefer. Allocate them categories in the following way:

- **Trash:** This one is for all the stuff you are going to be throwing out. This needs to be emptied the moment you have finished your task for the day.
- **Sell:** This rather exciting box is to be filled with goodies that will generate cash. I recommend waiting until the end of the process before selling.
- **Recycling:** This box is for items that need to be given to charity, recycled, or returned to their rightful owner.
- **Repairs:** This is for any items that need fixing, altering or completing in some way. Be realistic if you will actually repair these items.
- **Relocate:** As you progress, you'll realize things that are not in their correct 'home' – in other words, in their rightful place. All items that belong somewhere else should be placed into the 'Relocate' box. It is much easier to dump them here than getting up and making your way to another room, and then finding a place for them there. Stay in the area you are clearing to make the process easier, save time and to stay focused.

Ideally, you need to clear the last three boxes out at the end of every week to prevent them getting out of hand. If you find that on any given day they get too full, then of course you can take action – put things in your car so that you can take them to be fixed, move objects to their rightful place in your house and recycle.

Every room has a function

When in any given space, be vigilant about remembering the overall function of that space. What is its main purpose? Everything you decide to keep in that space, from furniture to knick-knacks to practical items, need to support the main function of that room.

Every object has a home

What do I mean by this? Ideally, every single item that you own (as far as humanly possible, anyway) has a proper place – its own 'home'. This allows you to find it easily in the future. Once your entire space has been cleared of clutter, you only ever need follow one rule:

> Once you've used something,
> simply put it back where it belongs.

It gets easier and easier once you start noticing when things are not in their rightful place. The same goes for filing. When paper is where it is meant to be, it requires no effort to find it when you need it again. Its 'home' should be a logical place that allows you to be proactive and efficient in locating it and using it later. At the end of Day 28 you will automatically know where all of your possessions are. Going forward, it takes not an ounce of time, effort or energy to locate something. You could even be out of your house or office and know 100% where something is located, filed or stored. Of course, this also means that your staff and everyone at home is on the same page as to where something lives. No more excuses. What a wonderful thought, and one we will be bringing into reality!

Like with like

Think about the concept of keeping 'like things with like'. Grouping items together so that things are more ordered in their placement is a very useful way to maintain a clutter-free environment. For example, keep your entire DVD collection together, medicines with medicines, linen with linen, and plugs or batteries in the same drawer.

Bear this idea in mind when working through the course. My aim is for you to create free space in your head and heart to be doing something far more *fun* and effective with your time than wasting it on looking for things. Remember the figure that jumped out at you from the calculator screen? The one that showed you how much money you're wasting by wasting time? Well, no more!

Store for retrieval

When you're deciding how to repack items you have chosen to keep, use the 'like with like' rule as a starting point. Then think about where you would most naturally want to look for the item when you think about it. With specific areas, such as clothing, kitchen appliances and toiletries, for example, keep things that you will need most often in the handiest place to reach. And then use the back of cupboards or space higher up for items you only require every now and then.

No mess morph

Use small wicker, plastic, woven, wood or paper cardboard boxes, containers or baskets to keep smaller items together and prevent 'mess morph'. Loads of smaller containers keep an area tidier for longer, making it easier to place things back in their home.

Music

Sound is an awesome accompaniment to clearing out clutter. If you find one particular area harder to tackle, choose music that will energize and 'funk' up your mood. If the job is more contemplative, such as when you clear out your desk or books, then play more mindful, easygoing music. It can be a fun element to go through lots of your music – and may even help you toss CDs that you will never listen to again!

> *Kate makes clutter cleaning easy by breaking up a huge job into bite-sized chunks. Tidying a bedside table is easy ... it's manageable. Waking up to a tidy space next to me was refreshing and inspired me to begin the next task and then the next. The reminder that medicines and beauty products have a shelf life meant that there was no attachment to all those icky bottles lurking beneath the sink in my bathroom cupboards. When it came to clothing, linen and books, just knowing that my once-loved items could be re-homed with someone else who may now have use for them made it easier to part with items I'd lugged around with me from home to home. Buying specific containers to house items*

not used daily helped me find things quicker, thus saving me time – and money – as I no longer needed to dash out to replace things I couldn't find. Getting the garage cleared out required the help of a strong handy man – but even that is now clutter free. Freeing up space in my house resulted in me being more organized. Everything now has a place and the house feels completely different.

Regards,
Brigitte Holmes

The physical process of clutter clearing

Here is the actual practical process to follow, as you start clearing out your nooks and crannies. Keep the following in mind as you tackle your first project.

- **Remove:** Get rid of all the items from within, on top of, behind or around the area you are clearing. *Completely!*
- **Clean:** Do some form of cleaning – even if it is just a quick wipe with a dustrag.
- **Decide immediately:** As you pick up each item to assess what to do with it, decide on the spot what you need to do with it. Handle each item just *once*. There are three vital questions to ask, which will help determine your choice:

> 1. Do I honestly *love* it?
> 2. Is it really *useful*?
> 3. Does it add *energy* and *value* to my life?

Dear Kate,

*I have tackled other areas and have found the [question], 'Does this add value to my life?' the most amazing tool to help me to de-clutter. I find that, surprisingly, I know the answer immediately and if the answer is **No**, I just chuck it! It almost gives me permission. An example is a number of things in my drawer that could only be used for long* *hair, including those ghastly banana clips. I have no intention of ever having long hair again, so they add no value to my life and out went a **bag** of stuff. If I hadn't used the 'add value' tool, I probably would have held on to them. I have been amazed at how much stuff I was able to throw out.*

Michele

So think of it like this: If you answer *Yes* to all three questions, simply decide if this space is the correct 'home' for it or whether you need to place it in your 'Relocate' box to live elsewhere in the house. If you love it, it but can't answer *Yes* to the last two questions, what are you really keeping it for? Be honest and ruthless as you evaluate all your possessions, and remember that we are making way for the *new* and *fresh* to come into your life.

- **Allocate:** If you decide to keep an item, clean it and either put aside to pack back into the space when the process is complete, or put it in the 'Repairs' or 'Relocate' box. If it needs to go out, it will land up in the 'Trash', 'Sell' or 'Recycle' box.
- **Complete:** The rule is that you have to complete an area 100%. Once you are done sorting and are left with the right items to be stored in the area you have just cleared, you are ready to put the items back. Remember 'like with like' and store for easy use or retrieval later in smaller containers, drawers or shelves. Throw the trash away – and you're done for the day!

Remember:

> Today I am letting go of XYZ, which no longer serve me, in order to make space for _____.

(Fill in what you wish to manifest, such as 'exciting new clients'.)

Day 2 - Bedroom (Part 1)

'Nothing is particularly hard if you divide it into small jobs.' – Henry Ford

Hooray! At last we get to today's actual task. I promise that from now on there will be less and less for you to read, so that your daily time is spent on clearing your clutter! Each day I will outline the *ideal* versus the *non-ideal* aspect of the space we are working with in order to highlight it from both positive and negative points of view.

The bedside table

To get you started, we're doing two small areas today. The reason we are starting here is because your bed is the place where you revitalize and replenish your energy every night as you sleep.

Your bedside table is not your local dumping ground. When you open and close your eyes, the space next to you needs to be open and clear and make you feel good inside. It has to lift your spirits immediately, not drain you in any way.

IDEAL: CLEAR AND SIMPLE SPACE

Your bedside table or nightstand with drawers should ideally house items you absolutely need when you are in bed. The top may hold the *one* book or magazine you are currently reading, your cell phone (not the most ideal place to keep your phone because they emit negative frequencies, but is often necessary nowadays), a lamp, a glass for water and any medication or vitamins you take daily. It may also hold something that lifts your spirits, be it spiritual material, your journal or an object of beauty that inspires you.

Inside your nightstand or in a pretty basket below or on a shelf there may also be a few further items used only in the bedroom – perhaps a manicure set, other medication, hand creams, hairbrush, or sex aids. This is also where you may want to keep your watch and jewelry if they do not have another home, such as a dressing table or your safe.

NOT IDEAL!
Do not keep more than two books next to your bed. These tend to overwhelm the senses and add further pressure, usually making you feel bad, guilty and stressed when you look at the pile of unread material.

Do not keep your cell phone charger next to your bed either, because all the electrical activity is not too good for you – if possible, charge your phone in your study, second bedroom or den before you go to bed.

The rule of thumb is to not keep anything next to your bed that is not directly related to sleeping, rejuvenating your body or sex! The area is often a dumping ground for anything that erupts from your handbag or trouser pockets and becomes a mishmash of little things. Invest in drawer dividers to alleviate losing smaller items you wish to keep here, or a beautiful bowl for loose change, etc.

Under the bed

The rule is: Do not store anything under your bed!

IDEAL: **EMPTY SPACE**
The space under your bed should 100% free of anything! It can't be any simpler than that; sorry, but this is just the way it is, because you need the space, airflow and wonderful lightness that come from a clutter-free space.

NOT IDEAL!
Do you *know* how many cobwebs and dust bunnies collect among things hidden under your bed? Let alone the bugs that just love to sleep close to you and keep you cozy as you sleep! Dustmites, though microscopic, are real and many people are allergic to them.

The only exception is if you have a bed with drawers built into the base set. In this case, make sure you store only linen, pillows and blankets in this space, and today would be the time to tidy that out too. It also needs to go without saying that anything stored in there is put away clean and ready for use when you need it.

● ●

So those are the physical spaces you need to clear out today. Tomorrow we will jump straight into the next task … less to read and more to do! Don't be tempted to read ahead, unless you are going to *do* the task – face the task as you get to it.

> *My clutter … Wow, it was everywhere! My bedside table, my bathroom! Oh my hat – you would have thought I thought they were never going to make cream again the way I stockpiled. And clothes … so hard for me. I have been every size from an 8 to a 16. I never wanted to get rid of my thin clothes because I wanted to get back there, and when I was thinner I couldn't let go of my fat clothes, just in case. How sad was that! The first step of de-cluttering my bedside table was so liberating – starting small, and realizing I could let go of things and it was manageable; and then it was amazing how well I slept without all the clutter next to my head going to sleep and waking up to!*
>
> *Another place where I was so cluttered was my e-mail. Clearing that was wonderful – felt so much lighter and focused and not so overwhelmed by work!*
>
> *Carol-Anne M*

Day 3 – Bedroom (Part 2)

I *know* you enjoyed waking up next to a clearer space this morning and can already feel the tangible benefits of living with just a little less clutter. We are going to stay in your bedroom today (but not your wardrobe just yet – that'll happen later in the week once you're more into the swing of things).

Start with your own bedroom – the place where *you* sleep. If there is too much to tackle in one day, simply focus on the 'stickiest' part, the hotspot that bothers you the most and drains all of your energy. Begin with something you'll realistically be able to complete within your hour today. If you need any pointers, then keep reading –otherwise just get started …

By the end of this process, it ideally takes no more than 10 minutes to tidy any space in your home!

This is the aim for any space you live in – and it may be quite a challenge for some! But it is entirely possible when your life is clutter free, when everything is in its proper 'home' and you have established a good level of organization. The only exceptions could prove to be your garage or storeroom, and your living area the night after you've thrown a party …

Using the same formula as yesterday (remember the five boxes) and following the same plan, simply start attacking an area of your bedroom that needs to be addressed, or go for the whole room if you can.

IDEAL: YOUR HAVEN AND SANCTUARY

Your bedroom has a few important functions:
- It is where you rest and replenish through sleep.
- It rejuvenates, offering you 'me' time.
- It is where you dress to perfection for your day.
- It is where you attend to your personal hygiene, such as manicures and pedicures.
- It is where you read inspirational material.
- It is where you connect with loved ones.
- It is where you enjoy intimacy with your partner.

But remember to answer the three-part evaluation:

> 1. Do I honestly *love* it?
> 2. Is it really *useful*?
> 3. Does it add *energy* and *value* to my life?

Your bedroom needs a bed and bedside tables, maybe a lamp or two, possibly some seating, perhaps a clothing rack and anything else that uplifts and adds value to your sleeping space. Some beautifully arranged objects are also appropriate. If you have pets, there may also be a corner for them to share the space, but avoid at all costs their toys and blankets being strewn across the room. Remember the 10-minute tidy-up rule we're aiming for.

This is also the day to turn over or rotate your mattress, and to check the quality of your bed linens, duvets and pillows to see what needs to be replaced. Perhaps take stock and make a note of anything that needs replacing or updating.

Once you have completed your bedroom space, you will feel energized, lighter and excited to go to bed tonight.

NOT IDEAL!

Your bedroom is not a dumping ground for everything in your life. Even important work-day items such as your briefcase or calendar organizer do not belong in your bedroom, so be vigilant. I would also suggest that things such as gym equipment do not belong here either. And don't even get me started on having your office in your bedroom! It is bad enough that work infiltrates so much of our time and space due to cell phones and laptops nowadays, but to encroach on your down time … Unless you live in a studio or apartment that requires the sharing of space and what it is used for, try to keep the function of your bedroom very specific.

Doors

Do not clutter up the space behind your bedroom door with loads of items hanging up or dumped on the floor. These just obstruct the natural flow of energy. Rather reassign them to the proper cupboards. If you have to have things behind your doors from a space perspective, then at least hang some gorgeous multiple hooks – with only one item per hook.

Blanket chests

If you keep a blanket chest at the bottom of your bed, make sure that it is filled with bedroom-related items, such as linen, towels, blankets or perhaps treasured objects such as photographs. Ensure it is clutter free inside and that its surface does not become a dumping ground.

> **TIP:** Always make your bed the moment you get out of it in the morning, or at least after you have showered and dressed. Leave your bedroom in a positive state that will welcome you back in the evening after a long day out. And imagine if someone popped in unannounced: Would you be happy to take them into it (should they need to use your bathroom, for example)? Fill your energy reserves by keeping things beautiful for yourself.

Day 4 - Bathroom

Are you getting into the swing of things this week? It's fun letting go of all the stuff that no longer serves you, isn't it? Today, let's shift our focus to the bathroom.

With the first task of clearing out my bedside table, I was proud that I only have a lamp and some crystals on my stand and nothing under my bed, so I just got stuck into spring-cleaning my bedroom – even washed the windows and burglar bars. I must admit that it was a whole different story for the bathroom cabinet. I could not believe how many half-used products I keep. I did not even think twice: stuff I do not use everyday when straight to the bin. I felt great once I cleared out everything and steam-cleaned the bathroom.

Theresa

When considering your bathroom today, the primary aim is to keep only products and toiletries that are up to date and that you use regularly. Remember the *function* of your bathroom ... Yes, yes, I know we're not meant to talk about these things, but let's get real here! Your bathroom is where you do the following:

- Let go of the day's dirt and grime.
- Release internal digestive clutter.
- Get ready for the day in terms of personal hygiene.

Its function is a vital part of letting go every day ... and preparing for the new. So everything that lives in this space needs to be clean, hygienic and inspiring. I bet you've never even thought of it in this way before.

IDEAL: HEALTH AND HYGIENE

All toiletries and medicines kept in the bathroom need to be within their sell-by date and appropriate to your life now. Your bathroom cabinet, the medicine cabinet on the wall, the shelves under the sink and all the other stuff lurking in your bathroom – on the bath, in the shower or in other 'tidy-alls' – are to be assessed today.

I personally find that 'tidy-all' storage spaces generally tend to become a 'trash-all' space where you stash anything and everything. Take whatever is not 100% necessary out of the bathroom, and enjoy your open, clearer space. Clean and hygienic are what we're aiming for.

Ideally, within your cupboard space, you should keep toiletries on one side and medicinal items on the other; when you need to retrieve anything, you immediately know where it is. When organizing your toiletries, I group similar things together, so that I know what I have and don't buy duplicate deodorants or face and body products, for example, and keep them separate, either in different rows or in small organizers such as plastic or wicker baskets. There are plenty of storage items readily available at home stores or plastic shops nowadays. You may even want to think about creating a medicine box, using something funky and functional to store all your medicines together.

Remember the concept of 'like with like'? This is a great way to sort your medicine:

- stomach/digestive disorders together
- pain/cramp medications together
- emergency first aid (plasters and burn salves) together
- chest and throat medicines together
- alternative or herbal tinctures together.

NOT IDEAL!

Toiletry products that are more than a year old need to be tossed. The aim is to get to the stage where you don't have a lot of stock wasted in your cupboards. Do you really need 10 different types of conditioner? Rather rotate and buy fresh, using a better storage and buying system. Old stuff lurking in the back of a cabinet is not good (energetically or hygienically). Toiletries *do* go off and rancid – and what good would that do to for your skin? And sticky bottles and gooey tubes in your bathroom just clog up your energy. *Yuck!* Remember the clean-as-you go rule, and especially with products – if you're keeping them, at least wipe them clean, especially the lids, before you place them back on the shelf.

And, if like most people you have loads of little 'bits' left in the bottom of several jars and bottles, either dump them, gift them, combine them into one bottle or place them out somewhere 'in your face' so you see them and can use them up over the next few days.

> **TIP:** If you share your bathroom with youngsters or teenagers, know that they go through phases where having 10 of everything is quite normal as they try out the latest gums and gels and sprays. The best you can do is to keep their potions in a funky container so they don't morph everywhere.

Ladies

Ladies … your make-up! Be sure to assess its age and rancidity – the rule is that mascaras go out out-out-out after six months because bacteria can build up in the brush and cause infections. Make-up also can spoil (smell your products!), let alone out of date trend wise.

Contemplate whether you need to update your look with some new make-up. (Perhaps check out a new look for yourself by visiting a MAC counter or professional make-up artist to get some refresher tips that will update your appearance along with a new you.) Be ruthless with the gungy bottom of lipsticks you will never use and old make-up brushes. Make-up should not be more than a year old at most! (I hear your *Eek!*)

Gents

Assess the state of your razors, aftershaves, colognes and brushes, for example, and toss out what is no longer hygienic or appropriate.

TIP: While today is essentially a physical clutter day, the fact that we are in the bathroom raises a vital point. Your skin is one the amazing features of your body, because not only does it protect you, it is also one of the ways that your body detoxifies. So, either tonight or tomorrow morning, treat yourself to a fantastic body scrub.

If you've found some nice products lurking in a corner that are for this purpose, then use them. Ideally, unless you have very sensitive skin, you need to do the scrub before wetting your body so that it is more effective and the particles are a little rougher. If you don't have commercial body scrubs, here is the ancient technique (and the one I prefer):

> *In a bowl place 2–3 tablespoons of table salt and cover with good-quality olive oil (3–4 tablespoons). It will get quite pasty and mushy, without the salt dissolving. Stand in the bath, or ideally in the shower, and liberally rub and scrub over your whole body before you get wet. Pay attention to feet, heels, elbows and knees, and rub in circular motions. The only place to avoid is your face and neck. Use special products on these areas if you have them.*

Your skin will go all tingly and red as you boost the circulation. Then rinse off with water. When you step out of the shower, the oil will still be on your body, and will serve to moisturise your skin. Try it as an amazing home remedy.

Day 5 - Body, purse and handbag

Did you love your body scrub spoil? Looking after your skin is vital for your skin to breathe and let go of toxins, so I suggest you schedule a weekly treat! And remember to drink your 6-8 glasses (4 glasses as absolute minimum) of water, because we're going to take another look at physiological clutter today, and water is the starting point.

Body

Take another look at the clutter form you filled in earlier, and decide on your main body challenge, the one that adds huge amounts of toxins to your body. Look at the biggies such as coffee, tea, alcohol, fast foods, cigarettes, unnecessary pills (such as headache tablets) and lots of preservatives.

I am not going to ask you to cut anything that can be a huge shock to your system (you shouldn't do that without proper, professional supervision), but I *am* going to ask you commit to the following: Pick the main negative area and be 100% honest about how much you consume, and consider the real effects? Okay, do that now …

What do you feel able to commit to when it comes to toxins? Are you willing to halve the amount you consume, or perhaps eliminate it from certain times of the day?

I do need you to commit yourself to *something*, however small to begin with, just to give your body a bit of a breather. Don't rush. Take some time to consider this and to make the commitment to rid yourself of physiological clutter that no longer serves you … Perhaps even share what you will be doing with someone else so that they can help you stay accountable. This might be a good time to come and post in the online community to get some added motivation.

Apart from your body, today we also move onto a clutter task that is vitally important for abundance and how you express yourself when it comes to money and your finances. Once again, you need to employ the clean-as-you-go rule, so that not only is everything neat and ordered inside your bag, purse or wallet, but it also looks in better shape on the outside, showing that you care about what you carry with you.

Before you start, remind yourself once again of your *intention*, what your wish to *manifest* through the energy that will come from clearing your clutter.

Purse or wallet

Your purse or wallet is an outward expression of how you value your money. Empty it now, taking note of how you do or don't arrange things.

IDEAL: ORDERED AND SEPARATED

Ideally your 'money bag' needs to be ordered with change money separated from bills, so that your admin is easier. I suggest keeping your receipts separate so you can use them for tax purposes and bank reconciliations at the end of the month; it takes only a second longer in the shop to put your cash in one place and slips in another! Also make sure that your money is always neatly folded and placed mindfully in the correct pouch. No more stuffing notes hastily away.

Your purse or wallet also needs to be in tip-top condition so that it reflects a healthy approach to wealth and abundance.

NOT IDEAL!

Money should not be stuffed mindlessly into your purse without a moment's pause for respecting it. Broken zips, studs, fasteners, buckles and ripped fabric lining or simply very old and shabby are a total no-no!

> **TIP:** Place a jar on your desk or kitchen countertop where you can place all your loose change (this prevents your purse from becoming too heavy and breaking), and then on a monthly basis pop the change into a charity box, add it to your savings, or help a child understand the value of money.

Handbag, satchel or briefcase

Much the same as what applies to your purse or wallet applies to these items, whether you are male or female. Any item that you carry around with you as an extension of yourself needs to be cleared of clutter today.

IDEAL: THE FIVE-SECOND RULE

The rule is that you have to be able to locate anything in your bag or briefcase within five seconds! Ideally, you should know where everything is located within these items, so that if I asked you for something, you would not even have to think about where to find it. For example, where should your purse go? Your cell phone? Your toiletries, calendar or whatever it is that you need to carry around with you? Where does your pen live?

Employ the same rule that everything has its own home and give them a proper home within your bag so that it saves you time and effort when you need to retrieve something. Apply the same rule for your briefcase, always assigning specific 'homes' for specific work-related items. Make sure your papers and important documents are ordered and neat and do not include any paperwork that should be filed somewhere else. (And always have pens and paper ready at the drop of a hat for an important moment!)

NOT IDEAL!

Don't let your bag or briefcase make you appear unprofessional. Scratching in your bag for something you need can negatively affect your reputation, let alone waste time.

> **TIP:** Did you know that there are even handbag inserts commercially available that you can simply take out of one bag and pop into the next, all while keeping things in the same place? Check out your local storage or plastic goods store (fairly commonplace nowadays). At the very least, ensure that your make-up is in a separate bag and that you have compartments for other goodies.

I really didn't know what to expect, but this week was a nice surprise and an eye-opener. Every day I wake up, do the necessary tasks at home (like a hit-and-run), go to work, rush back home, prepare dinner, eat, go to sleep, and the next day is just the same!

But in my mind there is always the nagging thought of: I want to unpack my cupboards and wardrobes, clean and rearrange the shelves, throw away stuff, etc. It's just a pity that you can only do a few tasks here and there because there is not enough time! But now with this course I am forced to make time, although it really isn't easy to find it, and already I can see much more order and tidiness in my house.

Tersia B

Heads up! The next two days are dedicated to looking at your clothes – if this is a highly emotional and difficult area for you to clear out, or you can just never get rid of clothes (just in case you will wear them or fit into them again), *please* enlist the help of a trusted friend or ask for help from my online community. It can make it all so much easier when you can ask someone else's opinion and help.

Day 6 - Wardrobe (Part 1)

Today is the first of *two* days dedicated entirely to working through your wardrobe and clothes. In my experience with clients, this can be one of the hardest aspects to clear – for guys and gals alike – so you really just have to approach this from wherever you are at emotionally, and take it a step forward from there.

Committing the time to unclutter with the huge work commitment over the past two weeks has been the biggest challenge. The cool thing is the process has given me an outlet to almost vent some of the frustration and stress. It's also amazing how you can ponder over things while you clear the junk and it gets your head in order at the same time.

The most fulfilling clutter-clearing session I have had so far was in my closet. I have been holding on to so many clothes in a bigger size. I lost about 55 pounds last year and have doubted my ability to maintain the loss that I held on to all the big stuff – in case.

*Well, I decided this weekend that the time to let go is now and that I will keep the weight off because that's who I want to be and when I have finished **igniting my life** I will have lost the rest and reached my goal so the empty shelf in the closet is for the new stuff I will buy when I get to where I'm going.*

I really need to focus on the detox; I have been great with the water but need to cut out the quick-fix snacks and up my game. Watch this space – this is the week things come together!

Marlene

We are going to split your wardrobe into two parts – one for today and another for tomorrow. Today will be all about the clothing folded on your shelves or dresser drawers, as well as your shoes. Tomorrow we will focus on the hanging clothes. I trust that this will work for you, as it is usually too much to tackle all at once. You may even find that you need to tackle just one small area of your shelves or drawers today, depending on how much you have stored up over the years! Whatever you choose, be sure not to bite off more than you can chew unless you are willing to take more time. It can get worse before it gets better and at some point it's all going to look terribly overwhelming. Take a deep breath and simply continue, one item at a time.

Shelves and shoes

If you have clothes scattered in more than one room, I suggest you start with your main area of storage, usually in your bedroom. Grab your five boxes and the simple formula again, with one addition when it comes to clothing.

- **Remove:** Remove all the items from your shelves and drawers, as well as all your shoes.
- **Clean:** Do some form of cleaning.
- **Decide immediately:** Remember to handle each item just once and make a decision on the spot. Once again, be sure to answer the three questions to help you decide, but there is also an additional one for clothing.

> 1. Do I honestly *love* it?
> 2. Is it really *useful*?
> 3. Does it add *energy* and *value* to my life?
> 4. Have I worn it in the past six to 12 months? (If not, it's time to be ruthless.)

- **Allocate:** If you are keeping an item, set it aside until you have worked through all your clothing, or place in the 'Repairs' or 'Relocate' box. If it needs to go to someone else, put it in the 'Recycle' box, and of course toss all the stuff deemed 'Trash'.

Right at the start of the process, you decided what you wish to manifest for yourself, so hold this in your mind as you go through your clothes.

IDEAL: SENSE AND STYLE

You really love and wear everything in your closet or drawers within a six-to-twelve-month cycle and it suits your current lifestyle. Your clothes help you make the most out of who you are and accentuate your features. You feel sexy and attractive wearing everything in your closet. Right? Yes, guys, you too!

The reality is that people wear about 20% of their clothes 80% of the time. Be willing to not be one of these statistics. Look realistically at your closet right now and be honest. Come on, I bet that, unless you've done ruthless clear-outs on a regular basis, you're pretty darn close to that ratio. What about having fewer clothes that you really love and wearing them more often? Here are a few ideal tips towards reaching the *ideal*:

- Everyone can benefit from your old clothes, so pass them on. Selling old clothes or gifting them to people you know, street kids or charity shops is a great way to make space for some new clothes that really suit you.
- Ideally, you already know your preferential wardrobe style, based on your body shape, personal preferences and what does and does not suit you, and can ruthlessly throw out accordingly.
- If you are not 100% sure, then consider getting rid of old, tired, frumpy and unflattering clothes this weekend, and then perhaps getting some expert advice so that you know exactly what to buy going forward. Both men and women can benefit from this personalized approach, so that you get a wardrobe that works for all occasions.

- The rule of thumb is if you have not worn an item in the last six months, or definitely within the last year, it's time for it to go. Even if you are able to answer *Yes* to the first three evaluation questions, you may be conning yourself …
- At the very most, clothes that have not been touched in the last two years have to go! They really need another home that will love and appreciate them.
- Go for quality over quantity.
- If you are honest and you have something that you still love that can be altered appropriately so that it becomes wearable, then skip off to a tailor to adjust the item a.s.a.p.

NOT IDEAL!

When it comes to your wardrobe, there are plenty of points in today's *Not ideal!* list:

- Having too many of any one item can be as a result of pure laziness in terms of how you shop and not giving any prior thought about what already exists in your closet or drawers. Do you *really* need 10 T-shirts in the same color?
- From now on, shop for new clothes only when you are in the right mood. Going shopping with credit cards when you're feeling stressed, down or negative is a sure-fire way to buy the wrong things for the wrong reasons. Stop buying clothing to fill the emotional clutter hole.
- Keeping clothing just in case? In case of what? Get over it – and get rid of it!
- Clothes that no longer fit you? Toss them, and go buy clothes that flatter you as you are *right now*. Stop waiting to lose the weight or until you've developed your six-pack. You will feel so much better about yourself when you wear clothes that fit and flatter you. Give your small or big clothes to someone who can revel in them. (See note on altering items above.)
- Ten pairs of black boots? Those boots were made for walking – let it go, let it go, let it go!
- For hygienic reasons, do not pass on intimate undergarments to anyone else – trash or burn them.
- Consider whether you keep clothes as a crutch. Do they fill some emotional hole for you? Rather ditch the clothes and get real about your feelings; it's much better for your emotional wellbeing, as well as your wallet.

- If you insist on keeping clothes you don't wear regularly, at least ensure that they are stored properly, or the bugs and moths will get to enjoy them, and nature will get rid of them for you!

> **TIP:** Using cedar blocks with clothing works well, as does vacuum packing, or using suit bags. Respect what you choose to keep.

Organize your wardrobe

For today and tomorrow, you need to consider how you are going to organize all your clothing in a way that works well for you. There are three basic ways to start, so if you need some assistance, simply pick the one that suits your nature and your wardrobe.

1. Organize according to when you will wear it: casual, smart, black tie, gym.
2. Organize like with like: all short-sleeves shirts together, shorts together, jackets together, pants together, slops and sandals together.
3. Organize according to color: all your whites together, your blacks together, and other colors that you would generally wear together. This last one is a fun, creative way to tackle your wardrobe, especially if you dress according to your mood.

> **TIP:** Imagine that your closet doesn't have any doors, and that if anyone walked into your bedroom you would be proud of the space. If you do not personally pack away your ironed clothes, teach whoever does (your partner or hired help) to work according to your new method.

Have fun bringing your closet up to date and making space for some glorious clothes that perfectly reflect who you are *now*!

Day 7 - Wardrobe (Part 2)

Please come to our online community today and blog about your past week's highlights, successes and challenges when it comes to clearing – and post those *Before*, *During* and *After* photos.

How great was it to wake up to a clearer room, and open your closets and drawers and be welcomed by space and organization?

What a week. I now feel so proud of my bedroom – should have taken Before and After photos. Every time I walk past my cupboards, I open, look and smile. **A wonderful feeling! Thank you!**

AK

Hanging clothes

I trust that you have been managing to do all the daily areas suggested this week. If you have fallen behind on any of your allotted hours for this week, consider catching up today so that you can start next week complete and up to date. Respecting your commitment to self and honoring your daily hour is about improving your relationship with yourself.

And, talking of commitments, are you still managing with your 6-8 glasses of water every day? By now you should be already finding that your skin is clearer, your body feels lighter, and your kidneys are working much more effectively. Go grab your bottle before you tackle the second part of your wardrobe clear-out …

I won't repeat anything from yesterday, because it's all still valid: simply apply the same information to all your hanging clothes!

IDEAL: SPACE TO BREATHE

Make sure that your hanging clothes have space to breathe and hang neatly. If in any doubt as to whether an item is worth keeping, try it on and see how you look and feel in it. If you have lots of belts or ties or both, consider hanging hooks on the inside of the closet door to keep them tidy. You can also purchase special scarf or tie holders.

Any special items that you do not wear often, such as dress suits or evening gowns, need to be stored carefully to protect them.

NOT IDEAL!

Do not allow your clothes to be squashed up against each other without any space to hang neatly and breathe. Lack of order means you waste time looking for clothes, which means you will be wearing 20% instead of 80% of your clothes.

> **TIPS:**
>
> - Place all your hangers facing the same way on the rod. Not only does it look neater, but is also easier to access.
> - Use the same kind of hanger (be they all wooden, plastic or wire) to make it easy on the eye.
> - Ensure that each hanger has plenty of space for the clothing to hang properly. There is nothing worse than pulling out an item that needs to be ironed all over again.

I no longer collect clothes and keep them with their tags on for 10 years. I cleared my cupboards with my children, who are two girls who were also catching the hoarding syndrome. What fresh air in the house. I also do not go to [clothing stores] when I am depressed. I work in the garden and when I am tired I go to sleep.

Dadi Mangondo

Three years after Hein died I finally had the guts to clean out his clothes cupboard. Your course was what helped me finally get the guts to open the doors and start sorting through his belongings. It took me two days to do it as I was crying so much, and afterwards I felt as though a huge weight had been lifted off my shoulders. Your course helped me unclutter my head and take the bull by the horns and dig in. Thank you, Kate. You are an inspiration.

Davwyn

Day 8 – Body

You have officially done a full week of clutter clearing! I bet that you're feeling better already. What changes are you experiencing?

Take just a few moments to think about the past week. What feels better in your space and what looks better already? From feedback from thousands of clients, I can also guess that there is already a chain reaction in other areas of your life, as you evaluate everything with the definition of 'clutter is anything that no longer serves me'.

> I didn't think that, at the ripe age of 38 (note I didn't say old), I would discover things about myself. You move from day to day thinking you're in control but in reality I've just been going through the motions. I have realized that unless I have a goal to work towards I am just existing, not living.
>
> The uncluttering of my world has been refreshing but at the same time leaves me with a sense of unfinished business – so much more to clear. But I also realize that I can't achieve this overnight. But, hey, things didn't get this messy overnight either. One day at a time, plan, act and the control will come back. Water has become my new companion – I can't say it's an easy transition, but I persevere. I've been sharing the experience with my girlfriends and I find it helps me keep it real – nothing like making commitments to yourself publicly that you don't stick to. You can't say you're detoxing and then have the vino and pizza everyone else is. But when they see me sticking to my plan they are inspired to do the same. It's also great to get the feedback, support and encouragement.

So detox rolls out to the rest of the Urquharts – why should I keep all the goodness to myself? Besides, it makes things easier if everyone close to me is on the same page.

M Urquhart

It is now vital that, as soon as you have cleared an area of clutter, you give yourself every opportunity to *keep it ordered*. Remember that it should only ever take you about 5–10 minutes to clear up any room that has been organized, and now you can count your entire bedroom and bathroom as on that list already! When things have a home, you no longer have to think about where to put them, and it takes nanoseconds to put something back where you found it. This is the only rule going forward!

Back to the boxes

Before we move ahead to this week, we need to just take a moment to check the boxes. If for any reason you didn't get around to them during the week because you were itching to move on, it might be useful to take action on them right now.

Some tips you could follow:

- **Trash:** Hopefully, you've been throwing out the rubbish generated from any given area immediately to signal the final end of that task.
- **Recycling:** Choose some things from this box – even if you can't do it all – and get the items to wherever you wish to send them. You can even call up charity shops and they will collect from you. This will save you time and effort. If any of the items belong to someone else, make the call today to arrange their return.
- **Repairs:** Take constructive action today, even if it means making a phone call to book an item in for repair, or to actually do it or plan to do it yourself.
- **Relocate:** If you haven't already placed these items in their appropriate home this week, do so today. If the place where it needs to go is not yet sorted and cleared of clutter, rather leave it in the 'Relocate' box for now.
- **Sell:** I suggest you do this task at the very end of the process.

A few things to note

This book is about letting go of all the clutter that no longer serves you: once you have let go of a lot of the 'stuff' you have been hanging onto for all the wrong reasons, the next natural step would be to think about new ways of organizing what is left. Occasionally, I give you tips on how to think about organizing or storing things differently. However, our focus here is getting *rid* of stuff first, because that is the most crucial step and when left with what matters most people seem quite capable of sorting it into a system that works for them. For specific help in a particular area not covered, ask me on the online community. If we just focused on organizing and not clearing, then you would be left with loads of organized clutter that would still not serve you.

Remember that clutter can be physical, body or emotional and all three have very similar negative impacts in terms of keeping you stuck and unable to embrace anything new into your life.

The reality is that you started reading this book because you are in touch with your yucky space and physical mess, let alone wasted time – or the general sense of overwhelming that comes with too many things to tackle and no idea how to wade through all the clutter.

As you spend your time, energy and effort on letting go of more and more every day, you may already be finding that the inspiration of spring-cleaning is positively affecting everything else too. So even though we're not yet specifically targeting the unresolved emotional and energetic aspects, the process may just be starting to evolve naturally for you and you may find that you are already having different conversations with people. Some of the first conversations may revolve around emotional differences in terms of your living space, especially if you share your home with others. Your de-cluttering process may thus be affording you opportunities to talk to others about how things happen in your home.

Remember to be open and willing to let energetic (emotional) clutter start shifting too. This starts happening naturally. As you clear one aspect of your life, the next one starts clearing itself out too. Think of it as the powerful, positive knock-on effect of clutter clearing working its magic in your life.

Great, now we can get onto today's task …

We need to take another step in de-cluttering the physiological body clutter. We've already started with the most important habit of drinking water, and then you did a body scrub (to slough of old, dead skin and awaken your body). We also looked at reducing one of the toxins that you regularly consume, and you should already be putting this into action.

So today I want to mention each of the different areas you need to consider, as well as the options that are available. I suggest that you read the following, and then go and chat to someone in the know at either your health store or pharmacy about some options that may suit you best.

I'm challenging you to pick at least two things from the list below. This will help you in taking the next step to help your body get rid of some stuff that no longer serves it.

Skin

I recommend that you get a body brush product for dry-body brushing. These are special brushes made from sisal (cactus) and are used before you wet your body. Do note, though, that some of the cheap varieties are made from nylon and therefore *not* suitable. Body brushes are a great, inexpensive product for eliminating skin toxins, as well as speeding up your blood and lymphatic circulation. They serve to energize and invigorate you.

Kidneys and lymphatic system

- There are great products that help your organs eliminate waste more effectively. For many of these products, you simply add to water and drink daily, so they are easy to take. You will definitely start urinating more frequently and should lose that bloated or heavy feeling.
- Get some essential oils to add to your bath, or to rub into your body after showering. This is a great way to detox. Choose oils that suit your needs, but make sure that you know how to use them properly. If in doubt, buy ready-mixed ones and get rubbing or soaking.
- You could also opt for herbal tinctures, as well as homeopathic remedies. Ask for advice, and choose what makes you most comfortable.
- Herbal teas work wonders too, especially green tea or fennel tea.

> **TIP:** Always ask a professional in your area for advice and, if you have any medical conditions, be sure to consult your doctor first.

Bowels and colon

- You have to start thinking about how your body eliminates waste, even if it is not so pleasant to think about. Yes, I know that many people have issues thinking about, let alone acting on this aspect of clutter! This is one area that tends to embarrass people, but you just have to get over it and say it like it is! The bottom line is that everyone has dead waste building up in their colon, and we need to get rid of it to ensure maximum absorption in the gut, as well as maximum elimination … Think of it as extra space in your body and definitely as getting rid of stuff that no longer serves you!
- While increasing your intake of water, fruit and veggies will help, there are also special remedies you can take that will help your colon to de-clutter more effectively. My favorite is a product that combines 17 different herbs. Products such as this will get you regular, and get rid of old waste cluttering up your body. You mix these with water (I prefer juice) as they are a little difficult to swallow.
- An alternative to the branded products available is plain psyllium husk powder. You can also soak a handful of linseeds in water overnight, and take them in the morning. They can be a bit 'slimy' once they've been soaked, but I love them.
- You can also get a product on the market called Detox patches. You apply them to your feet at night.

Exercise

- Some form of exercise is vital. It may simply mean running up every flight of stairs from now on, but you have to get your body moving if you're not already doing so.
- If you are not in a proper exercise routine, then walking is the very best way to get your body moving. It costs no money, and just a little effort. Start with 5–10 minutes every day if this is what you choose. But commit to it daily.
- Yoga is a great way to get rid of stress and tension, as well as toxins in your body. I personally do Bikram yoga as it helps regenerate my spirit while squeezing every ounce of toxins from my body through sheer sweat and forces me to look at emotions for every minute I stand in class. Find what works for *you*.

> **FACT:** Employees who exercised before work or during lunch breaks were better able to handle the day's demands. Their general attitude also improved.
>
> - 72% reported improvements in time management on exercise days
> - 79% said mental and interpersonal performance was better
> - 74% said they managed their workload better
> - 27% experienced higher levels of concentration at work
> - 41% experienced higher levels of motivation to work
>
> – University of Bristol, Department of Exercise, Nutrition & Health Sciences, in *International Journal of Workplace Health Management*, 2008, Vol. 1, Issue 3

IDEAL: REDUCE!

If you're looking to detox, it's best you eliminate or at least reduce the following from your diet:

- coffee and tea
- animal proteins
- sugar (such as chocolate, for example …)
- processed food
- sauces and other rich foods
- preservatives and colorants
- anything that makes you moody, irritates your stomach or reduces your energy levels.

IDEAL: INCREASE!

Do yourself a favor and increase your intake of the following:

- water
- fresh fruit
- fresh vegetables (can be cooked, just preferably not frozen)
- plant protein
- beans and pulses
- grains (such as short-grained brown rice, for example).

To summarize, you need to keep up with your first body detox commitments from last week, and then pick two things from the aforementioned list. Now get going … find some time to get out there and get cracking.

> **TIP:** If you're battling with carrying a large bottle of water with you, get three small ones. Keep one next to your bed to drink in the morning and night, one on your desk for the day and the last in your car or your handbag. This way you will definitely get through 6 eight ounce glasses a day.

Day 9 – Kitchen (Part 1)

For today's task, as a follow-on from the physiological clutter we focused on yesterday, you are moving into the kitchen.

Fridge and food

Start off with your fridge, because this is where food is more likely to be out of date, especially perishables.

IDEAL: FRESH AND ENERGIZING

- Remove everything from your fridge and give the space a cleaning with some good disinfectant that you can use around food. If in doubt, use a small amount of dishwashing liquid on a damp cloth. If you can, pull the fridge away from the wall so you can clean out underneath and behind it. And while you're at it, clean the very top too! It almost always gets forgotten in anyone's cleaning routine.
- It is vitally important that your fridge is spotless – because this is where much of your nourishment comes from.
- As you go through each item, assess its freshness and expiration date. Discard all outdated products immediately.
- Clean the sticky goo off the top of sauce bottles – that means opening them too and cleaning inside the lid.
- When repacking, place like with like – in other words, all your sauces, jams, or pickles together so that they are easier to find when you need that instant snack.
- Unless it's frozen in the freezer, meat should be stored in the bottom half of the fridge to prevent blood spilling onto and contaminating other food by accident.
- Obviously religious requirements regarding foodstuffs will override how you store food.

- Your fridge is now clean and fresh and smells great! It is well stocked with items that are fresh, healthy and within their expiration date.

NOT IDEAL!

Avoid at all costs:

- old or stale products
- anything past its sell-by date
- manky fruit and veg
- grubby sauce bottles with black rims around the top

Freezer

Go through your freezer and make a note of anything that is nearing its sell-by date and needs to be eaten as soon as possible. You could even make it a household rule that you eat everything in it before you restock.

If you have an older fridge that needs manual defrosting, then this would be the perfect day to do it, and get rid of some newspaper at the same time.

Food cupboards

As with the freezer, you could make a point of eating and using up most of your foodstuffs before you rush off and replenish them. That is a great inspirational act of spring-cleaning!

Do you have enough storage containers for all your items, or do you need to purchase more so that your food cupboard is a little more organized and streamlined? Having matching containers can make storage easier on the eye, and may add to the sense of achievement.

IDEAL: FRESH AND ENERGIZING

All the same rules for the fridge apply here too.

NOT IDEAL!

- Be vigilant about whether you have overstocked cupboards out of sheer habit, especially when it comes to items you seldom or never use, even if your grandmother says you should …

- Make sure foodstuffs such as flours and grains do not have weevils or other bugs.
- Take note of how much junk food or unhealthy options there are in your cupboards at the moment. Perhaps you could start thinking about shopping more consciously, because the less junk food (read 'clutter') you have stashed away, the less likely you are to eat it.

> **TIPS:**
> - Always place like with like.
> - The items you need or use more often should be stored in an accessible place so you do not have to rummage through the whole cupboard every time.
> - The neater and tidier your cupboards, the more likely you will know what is in them, and then you will not have to buy duplicates unnecessarily.
> - You can also get shelf extenders – such as an additional wire rack (ideal for cans) that effectively doubles your shelf space.

Well, after the chat I had with Kate on Tuesday, I had a long hard talking to myself. You see, I made excuses for not following the detox 100%, but after the chat I realized that I was given this fantastic opportunity to better myself and not only am I letting myself down, but also Belinda who made this happen and Kate for giving her time. So I gave it my all, the only time I fell down was Friday after a meeting. I had three sticks of dried sausage, but I stayed clear from all the pastries and mini pies. I even got myself a small teacup for my coffee (still on three cups a day). Green tea and water are my new friends now.

My headaches from cutting down on coffee only went on Saturday. So glad about that. I am taking food on the road now and eat between store visits.

I realized that I tend to make excuses for bettering myself but will always do everything for work – how sad is that? There will come a time that if I don't look after myself

I will not be able to do great at work. So from now on I will give 100% to the detox program, as just in this short time of correct eating I feel so much better.

I booked myself for a foot massage next week Monday – looking forward to that.

So now that my new motto is 'What I put in is what I get out', I cannot wait for next week to start. I am ready and committed.

Theresa

Day 10 – Kitchen (Part 2)

Did you enjoy going to your fridge this morning and finding a nice cleared-out space awaiting you? Was there even anything left?

When you are doing your daily tasks, remember that how much you manage to get through in your allotted hour always depends on how much clutter you started with in the first place. Simply do what you can, and let it be, unless you specifically want to do extra time in any area. But remember that taking two hours to do something today does not mean you can forgo tomorrow's task! All areas are vital …

Dishes, cutlery and appliances

Today we are staying in the kitchen and focusing on your crockery, cutlery and appliances. Chances are you have things lurking in those cupboards and drawers that you never use, and you could dump, sell at your local buy-and-sell cash-conversion store or even online, recycle or repair so that everything in your kitchen is in *use*.

The exceptions to the 'daily use' rule would be your special second set of dishes or cutlery if you have one. Just make sure that these are stacked and stored properly, and that you store them at the back of your cupboard so they are not in the way of everyday access to readily used items.

IDEAL: **LOVED AND USED**

- Your everyday dishes and cutlery is within easy reach, and it is all in good shape. There should be no chips or cracks! If there are, throw them out right away. The energy from damaged goods will sap your own, never mind the germs that lurk in the cracks …
- All your appliances add value to your life and make cooking an easier or more enjoyable experience.
- Remember the all-important formula you used for your wardrobe and implement it ruthlessly in the kitchen, adding a fifth evaluation question:

> 1. Do I really *love* it?
> 2. Is it really *useful*?
> 3. Does it add *energy* and *value* to my life?
> 4. Have I used this in the past six months?
> 5. Does it have any chips or cracks?

- Take a good look at your countertops. Is there too much stuff lurking there and do you need to put some things in the cupboards to simplify the space again? When you walk into your kitchen it should feel clean, airy and light, with heaps of space to prepare food.

NOT IDEAL!

- Do not be tempted to hang on to 50 different gadgets and other supposedly 'useful' appliances that never see the light of day. As with clothing, if you have not used it in the last six months, then why would you start now? Get rid of them, donate them, or better yet, sell them for cash.
- I'm am afraid that even if you answered *Yes* to the first evaluation questions, when it comes to things that you cook in, eat off or eat with, there is *no* room for chips and cracks. They are a breeding ground for bacteria. Let them go! You may have to wait a week or two till payday in order to replace a broken pot, but at least make a note that it must go as soon as possible.
- Obey the 80/20 rule – 80% of your countertop is clutter free, thus freeing up space on which to work. Most households get lazy about putting stuff away, and have 80% of the spaces filled with clutter. Be ruthless.
- Keeping lots of mismatched items from different dishes or cutlery sets can be very draining. Unless you are into the eclectic look or boast an impressive collection of vintage or antique pieces and truly love the quirkiness they offer, then perhaps you've been hanging on to them long enough. Get rid of them and rather buy one new, complete set that you love. Gift the mismatched ones to a community center or

charity, and let someone else who is just starting out in their own flat, such as a student, enjoy them. Remember you are making room for the new to come whizzing into your life.
- Keep your intention top of mind, by repeating it as you clear out:

> Today I am letting go of XYZ, which no longer serve me, in order to make space for _____.

> **TIP:** To keep your countertops tidy, conveniently place one nice bowl or an interesting tray where you can dump bits and pieces as you come into the kitchen. Often we go to the kitchen first when we come home (we need a cup of tea, we use the back door, or we carry shopping bags in from the car) and if items such as the mail, cell phone, a handbag, keys and your calendar don't have a designated space, you will dump them anywhere, and then waste time looking for them later.
>
> If you have a 'hotspot' that is designed to collect all these things, you will always know exactly where they are. Try it and see if it helps … Just remember not to make it too big, and to keep an eye on it in case too much stuff lands up in there and it needs to be relocated back to its real 'home'.

I no longer buy dinner plates and serving dishes. I only have one decent set in the house now and nothing in boxes. This has also helped me to say no to people who would unceremoniously rock up and expect me to cook for them. I have more time to myself for reading and sewing, as those are my hobbies. Standing in the kitchen doing the dishes is not mandatory routine any more. With all this I feel good, look well and am having a ball of a time.

Didi Mangondo

Day 11 – Books and magazines

While clutter clearing can be a tough job physically and an even tougher one emotionally, it is still obligatory to have some fun during the process of letting go. Right at the beginning I suggested that music was a great accompaniment to clutter clearing. If you have not used it at all, why not try it today because it leads directly to tomorrow's task anyway!

Books

Can you see how music might help this area of letting go? It can be such an interesting experience going through all your reading material while listening to music that may enhance the process for you. Remember your possessions have to inspire and energize you.

IDEAL: LOVE THE BOOKS YOU OWN
- Everyone has a different relationship to books – for some they are purely for pleasure, for others reference works; others collect books on specific topics; or you could simply choose to invest in an entire library of your own. There are no rights or wrongs, other than that you love what you keep. All the same rules apply.
- Books can feed your soul – or simply be lumps of paper collecting dust. Nowadays, with the advent of e-books and audio books, you may not have many physical books in your possession – I recently did another mammoth clear-out of magazines and books, thus clearing another layer so to speak in an already minimalist life. In 2012, I was down to 30 precious books that I chose to have in my life. As for the rest, when I wish to locate information about something, I do, but I do not have to own it. Be one of those people who adore *all* the books they have in their home or office and keep nothing out of obligation.
- If you're a serious book collector, this would be a slightly different task for you today, because your books may have a lot of sentimental *and* monetary value. If this is your situation, then perhaps today could be about clearing them, dusting them, and ensuring they are properly organized or valued, for example. For the rest of us, books are living things that love being used and read. Is a book even a book if it is never opened and read, passing its wisdom onto you?
- Make sure that you clean your books as you sort through them, because dust can damage them – and dust brings bugs …

- Organize your books according to whatever works for you – size, category or area of your interest, for example.
- Most importantly, your books need to be appreciated. Place some of your favorites on display on your coffee table so you are more likely to utilize them.
- Keep the books you want and relegate the others to one of your boxes, but I would never suggest throwing *any* books away. There is *always* someone who needs books. Sending them to a school is a great way to help with the ongoing education of children, and they can make a huge difference in someone else's life. If they are not the type of books suitable for children, then what about an old-age home, church or hospice? Even your local library will accept them and sell them in fundraising efforts to keep the library well stocked for the benefit of your own community.
- Remember to use the original three-point evaluation for books:

> 1. Do I really *love* it?
> 2. Is it really *useful*?
> 3. Does it add *energy* and *value* to my life?

NOT IDEAL!
- If you have gathered lots of other people's books, place them in your 'Recycle' box and get them back to their owners. The same applies to the books that you have lent to someone. Get them back because this can lead to energetic clutter, where there are too many loose threads in your life. If something is owed to you, then get it back.
- Don't keep books out of guilt – who does that serve?
- Do not keep every single novel you have ever read. Chances are you have moved beyond the favorite you read in high school.

> **TIP:** I just love second-hand bookshops! And they will happily take your second-hand books; some also take CDs and give you cash or credit to buy more books of your choice. What a cool win-win situation.

Magazines

I bet you also have piles of magazines lurking in some unsuspected corner of a room? Magazines tend to represent the promise of tasty treats you'll conjure up one day, exotic vacation, inspirational articles, financial acumen and staying abreast of your industry news – we all tend to keep a few just in case. Or more than a few! Today is a great day to be ruthless, applying the same rules as for books. If you really want to keep that recipe (and intend to use it), tear it out and file it in a binder and store it in sight in the kitchen. If you are genuinely a devoted gardener, then why not create a *Gardening tips* folder or start your travel destination vision board. Hospitals, clinics, libraries and schools will gladly take your unwanted magazines.

As a rule of thumb, unless you are making them an aesthetic statement of art in a certain space, I suggest you do not keep any magazines older than a year.

Hey, Kate

Loving my new space – and guess what? My teenagers are suddenly getting agitated with their mess! How fantastic is that? I am thrilled. My messiest one of all is suddenly cleaning cupboards and giving stuff away. Thanks!

Kim Ballantine

Day 12 – Music

Before we get stuck into today's task at hand, it's time to ask you once again how you're doing with your physiological clutter. Take a minute to honestly reassess the last few days and how you are *really* doing? These are the aspects we should have concentrated on and committed to so far:

- A daily water quota of 6-8 glasses
- Body scrub last week and scheduled for every week going forward
- Reducing your intake of toxins
- Embracing at least two body-clutter areas

Rate yourself out of 10 – with 10 being 100% on track and doing what is required of you and 1 being not at all. Are you happy with your current rating?

If you are not happy with your current situation and it is clear that you have been sidestepping these clutter projects, you need to take responsibility by doing something constructive. There is no point bemoaning your situation and then not taking positive action. You are required to take 100% responsibility and accountability for your life, and what you wish to change. Refer to your assessment score to get a gentle reminder. You will be rewarded with energy, vitality and more bounce in your step, all of which add value to the rest of your life and what you wish to manifest!

If you are not managing to take sufficient positive action on the suggestions made, perhaps you can enlist the help of someone else for more support? You could see a professional for a detoxification massage, a dietitian, reflexologist, a personal trainer to get your exercise routine going, or perhaps even treat yourself to a body-wrap to stimulate your circulation. There are always other options, but excuses are not one of them. So up the ante and get on top of it today!

Right, moving on …

CDs

When you cleared out your books and magazines yesterday, I suggested using music to enhance your experience, and hinted that it would lead to today's task. In fact, you might have already started clearing out …

Just as it is with books, we can get very attached to music. But if we never go through it all and assess whether this is still something we enjoy now, the CD collection simply expands and gets out of control, year after year. And yet we never listen to a quarter of it! The same rule we applied to clothing, applies here – we listen to 20% of our music 80% of the time. Maybe it's time to shift that percentage?

Nowadays, most people store their music on iPads and iPods, and sometimes even on CDs. Some of you may still be using tapes or even LPs. Today is for sorting through wherever you personally store your music.

> ### IDEAL: THE FIVE-SECOND RULE
> - The real test is: Are you able to locate any music you choose in five seconds?
> - Ideally, your music should be well categorized in a way that works for you, be it via category or alphabetically.

- You love every artist and album that you own, listening to it at least once every 6–12 months (the same as the clothing rule).
- After you have removed all your CDs from where they are stored and have given the space a wipe, start sifting through what you own and be honest, asking once again:

> 1. Do I really *love* this?
> 2. Is it absolutely vital for me to *keep* it?
> 3. Does it add *energy* and *value* to my life when I listen to it?
> 4. Have I listened to this in the last 6–12 months?

- Check that your CDs are in the right boxes – there is nothing worse than finding the cover you want, only to be confronted with a different CD inside.
- Think about recycling unwanted CDs by selling them to a second-hand shop for cash or credit to put towards music you would love to own now. Alternatively, you can also gift music to friends you know would appreciate it or even transfer them all to an MP3 format so you can have all your music in your car, for example.
- Because our music system is usually an integral part of our living area and this is a communal and commonly only used area, it might be cool to get your partner or kids (if your share your home with someone) to help you.

NOT IDEAL!
- Don't be tempted to keep music because you're just too lazy to go through it and make courageous decisions about what you need in your life right now.

> **TIP:** You could hold a barter party where everyone brings 10 CDs and 10 books to swop or sell. Cool way to pass it on or pay it forward!

iPods and MP3s

Double check all your downloads and streamline what you have saved. Ensure that you have appropriate back-ups, so that it is all in perfect order. There is nothing worse than losing everything stored on that nifty gadget, so rather be prepared for an unexpected loss of music – because it *can* happen.

Storage

When you have decided what music you are definitely keeping, you need to start asking if there is a better system of storage or organization than the one you have been using. You have to think about how you would retrieve them when you want to listen to them.

While MP3s and iTunes do it all for you, the same isn't true for hard copies. The less you have to think about where each CD is located, the less time and effort it will take you in future to find the one you want to listen to, and you'll also know where to place it in its proper 'home' once you have listened to it. Make sense?

The most popular ways in which to store music are:

- Alphabetically – either by first or last name of the artist or the group.
- Types or genres of music – classical, jazz, rock and modern, for example.
- According to how often you listen to them. So your favorites, the ones you always play, could be kept together, with less-used ones separate from them.
- By decade.

Day 13 – Memory lane

In my experience, memories are one of the hardest areas to tidy and clear of clutter, so muster up all the energy you can to tackle this one!

Our lives are represented visually by everything external to us – our home, the objects in our home, inherited goods, how we dress, our car, yet nowhere is our history more tied up than in our …

Photographs

Photographs have the ability to instantly uplift or to drain us. Although they are considered physical clutter because you can see and feel them, photographs also have an immense amount of emotional energy attached to them. They reflect our past, are evidence that we exist, prove that we have had a life, that we are someone and have come from somewhere.

Depending on your age, you may have several albums, or even a multitude of boxes stuffed with photos lurking somewhere. If you're techno-savvy, then yours may already be stored on your computer, on a hard drive somewhere or on disk.

IDEAL: FOR PLEASURE

- The photographs you are keeping are well preserved, stored and ideally scanned for longevity as well.
- You enjoy your favorite photos in frames and collages around your home so that they add warmth and vitality to your living space.
- Your photos are categorized into eras or events. When you want to take a trip down memory lane or a friend or someone in your family wants to see what, who and when from way back when, you know just where to find them. Easily and enjoyably.

NOT IDEAL!

- There are hundreds of photos all jumbled up and in no particular order.
- You've hoarded photos of events and people that remind you of a bad time.
- You still have photos you do not like, for whatever reason …
- Your photos are stuck together with the old glue or by water damage.
- Your photos are stuck in old albums that are yellowing with age.
- You still have the old packets with the pockets for negatives.
- All your photographs are loose, stuffed in drawers, boxes, hidey holes or in the garage – all getting irreparably damaged.

> **TIP:** Ask yourself whether you need to keep the negatives from 20 years ago.

Preserving the memories

When it comes to photographs, modern technology is our friend.

Choose your absolute favorite and most inspiring ones to be displayed in your home and office and then scan all the rest for your computer. That way you can scroll them as your screen saver or enjoy them in a digital frame. The most important thing to remember is to let your photographs enhance your life in every moment, adding a sense of belonging and vitality to your spirit, or there is no point in keeping them.

Not only will technology allow you to save space, but more importantly you will also preserve the integrity of the originals.

> **TIP:** It is easy and inexpensive nowadays to create fabulous works of art using canvases or digital photo books as coffee-table books. Celebrate your past and present by only having photos that inspire you!

Day 14 - Living space

Today is the day we move onto the bigger rooms in your home at last! But before we get onto today's task, I'd like to remind you that on some days you may have time on your hands after completing a task, and yet still not have spent your allotted hour of clutter clearing. Perhaps one area or task has no 'hook' for you; perhaps you have recently cleared it all out; or maybe it is simply an area where you are naturally well organized. If and when you find yourself with extra time on any given day, then I suggest you try one of the following:

- Go back over previous days to see if there was anything you missed.
- Revisit a task that you never got around to the first time.
- Hopefully the next day's task will introduce an area that you can join in with full gusto again.

Living room

This is your open, social space, the one you share with family, entertain guests, replenish at the end of the day and where you read, relax or party up a storm.

IDEAL: A REFLECTION OF YOUR PERSONALITY

In many ways, this space is the center of your home and is ideally a beautiful haven that energizes you when you walk into it. It will have both functional pieces (sofas and a coffee table) and aesthetic pieces (art, vases, candles, treasures) that all work together to create the amazing space you want.

Generally, you'll want to create some beautiful focal points. This does not mean that every single tabletop has to be crammed full. Make sure that the hour you spend today will leave your living room clearer, fresher and with at least a little more space. Read through the ideas below, pick what matters most to you, and get stuck in.

Your living room usually involves bigger tasks such as books, photos and CDs, which is why we did these over the past two days so that we have a head start on the bigger space.

When clearing your living room, you may want to shift furniture around for a new look that will instantly refresh the feel of the room and offer you a new perspective.

If you have storage units such as cupboards, chests and drawers then this would be the day to clear them out. Be mindful of what you are storing in these hidden areas – ideally each drawer has one purpose only.

Also check the quality of your cushions, throws, blankets, ottomans and sofas. Does anything need tossing, recycling, repairing or re-upholstering? Sometimes just changing the cushions or even the covers and displaying new colorful candles can positively impact a room immediately.

If you have plants, check whether they need repotting into bigger pots so they can breathe and grow again. Remove all the dead parts and even give the leaves a wipe. Yes, odd I know, but the leaves of indoor plants gather dust and then they can't breathe.

If you live with pets, make sure their toys, blankets and baskets are neatly in one area rather than scattered chaotically throughout the living room. And the same applies to the kids' stuff: keep handy (and decor relevant to the adult living space) storage boxes where all their toys can be tossed in three minutes flat. Teach young children to help you with this task and, as they grow older allow them to put toys away on their own. You could even make a game of it. If you always do it, you will always do it!

See what you can let go of to lighten up your living space. Depending on where your front door is situated, you may want to place some nice coat hooks for hanging coats, umbrellas and hats, for example.

NOT IDEAL!

- There are loads of scattered objects with no order.
- Messy piles of magazines have stacked up over time.
- Dirty cups and other trash have begun to accumulate.
- Your living space is filled with things that don't add value to the function and aesthetics of the room.
- Moths have attacked the blankets and throws.
- Toys for kids or dogs have erupted everywhere like a volcano.

> **TIP:** Here is one little tip you will love! It can be very useful to create one 'dumping drawer' in your house. But it comes with my three guiding rules too, of course.
>
> 1. It is the place where you put anything that does not have another proper 'home'.
> 2. It is fairly small – in other words, one single chest drawer.
> 3. It is cleared out regularly to prevent it from getting out of hand – at least every six months.
>
> Your best bet is to assign the dumping drawer to the living room (or even the spare room if you have one), as long as it is somewhere accessible because very often the stuff that's tossed in there is as a result of everyday living and has no real home. The dumping drawer means that if you ever are in doubt about where you might have or should put something, you have one spot. It will give you some sense of relief that there can be a chaotic drawer waiting for you when you need it!

So Week 2 is gone. I cannot believe how fast it goes.

The week started a bit slow but ended really well. The detox is going well, had a cell meeting and girls' night on Wednesday, a birthday on Saturday and today, and I stuck to the eating plan and I cut coffee to three cups this week. I must admit my skin feels better.

The best part is that my home is looking fab; I have a small townhouse and got rid of a lot of my extra furniture so

I had to store all my stuff, but now I got rid of most unused stuff …

I am learning to live without the 'just-in-case stuff' I used to keep. It just makes my life so much easier. Why have I not done this before? I am also so much more relaxed when I get home, knowing all is in place.

Well, I am looking forward to Kate's guidelines next week because with each week I feel better.

TJ

Day 15 – Dining room

Did you skip gleefully into your living room this morning knowing that you had cleared out some little area yesterday, if not most of the space? I hope you're reveling in the results of your hard work and appreciating all the shifts you have been making.

There is very little to read for today, so let's save some time. Everything relevant to the living room space applies to today's task area, with the possible addition of looking at your seating arrangements and where you eat. Your living room and dining room are fairly similar spaces and thus often share similar items.

IDEAL: WELCOMING HAVEN

This space should always be ready to welcome guests for a meal. As you clear your dining-room space today, imagine that at any given time guests can arrive and you will be able to seat them at the table for a meal. If you have a sideboard or any other type of similar storage facility in the room, it should be reserved for accessories that contribute to the function of the room, and contain cutlery, table linen, napkins, serving dishes and perhaps candles.

> **TIP:** Try to keep all your passages and doorways clear of clutter. This allows for maximum flow into and out of all rooms.

NOT IDEAL!

The dining room tends to be the space where everything is dumped on the table as you enter: laptops, groceries, school bags and pictures. Allocate a special place in the home for dumping, just *not* the dining table. If you are using your dining table as a desk, which does occur, then ensure you have a system in place that means you are able to put it all away quickly and easily, and can eat around the table in five minutes flat.

> **TIP:** Think of your home as a guest house! I am not suggesting that your home be 100% spotless and in order all of the time. But when you walk into your home, or any room in it, you should be proud that it is yours. Your energy lifts, not slumps, when entering the space. This also means that at any given time, someone could pop over unannounced and you would not be embarrassed, ashamed or feel compelled to make excuses as to why everything is in a mess.
>
> If you think of your home as a guest house, then you will start to see it through other people's eyes. If you are brave, it can be very useful to get a friend to lend their eyes to see it from a different perspective.

Day 16 – Office or study (Part 1)

The results of a survey among 400 of my clients revealed that the hardest areas to tackle are as follows:

1. Office – 26 %
2. Garage/storage – 21%
3. Living areas – 17%
4. Bedroom – 16%
5. Kids' rooms – 13%
6. Kitchen – 6%
7. Bathroom – 1%

We are dedicating plenty of time to your office or study so that you can tackle it 100% and never let this area run your life again! But, first, let's briefly recap some important things to remember before you begin:

- Every time you clear out your physical clutter, you have five boxes or bags with you, so that you can easily delegate the item to one of the areas.
- While you clear, keep in mind your initial intention, so that clutter clearing has a greater purpose.

> Today I am letting go of XYZ, which no longer serve me, in order to make space for _____.

- Drink plenty of water every day to ease the letting-go process and to stay well hydrated. Clearing clutter can be an emotional exercise and can take both a physical and emotional toll on your body.
- As we kick off the last week of physical clutter, take a few minutes of your hour to ensure you are shifting at least some of the items from the boxes in which you have been gathering things.

Back to the boxes

- **Trash:** Hopefully, you have been throwing out the trash generated from any given area immediately to signal the final end of that task.
- **Recycling:** Choose some things from this box, even if you can't do it all, and get the items to wherever you wish to send them. You can even call up a charity shop to collect, saving you time and effort. Actioning just one thing will make you feel fabulous.
- **Repairs:** Take constructive action today to tend to at least one item in this box.
- **Relocate:** If you haven't already placed these items in their correct home this week, do so today. Walk around your home, placing stuff where it rightfully belongs. Remember the concept that pretty much 'everything you own has a home'.
- **Sell:** Keep all these items until you have been through your whole home.

And now for today's specific task … Note that your office is split into two sections over three days. Today we tackle your desk space, and over the next two days your filing system.

Your desk

I suspect that, as a result of the lessons you have been absorbing and executing over the past two weeks, there may have been some natural shifts in how you keep things. Any tidier? As you look at your desk today, notice whether there have been any subtle changes lately?

When it comes to the space you work at every day, be it in an office at work or a study at home, you need to think about your energy. Contemplate the meaning of your work, specific outcomes and productivity. Are you able to find things effortlessly when you need them and is your work 100% up to date? When your desk is free of clutter, looks professional and is inspirational, then it is that much easier to feel positively compelled to work, to work well, and to work productively. This is true for the home executive paying domestic bills as well as a top executive running a company! A messy, cluttered desk just keeps your head fuzzy and your logic stagnant.

> **FACT:** In surveying 1 000 middle managers of large companies in the USA and the UK, 59% miss important information almost every day because it exists within the company but they cannot find it.
> – Accenture, *The Wall Street Journal*, 15 May 2007

IDEAL: A REFLECTION OF YOU

- Your desk reflects who you are and how you wish to work. You can find things immediately, and feel organized and in control of this space.
- Imagine leaving your desk 100% clear at the close of every single work day, so that when you see your desk first thing in the morning, your energy levels are elevated and you're keen and willing to get stuck in (just like you leave your bedroom the way you wish to come back to it every night)?
- Having some form of notice board, pin board or white board for reminders can be useful in keeping your work surface clear.
- Your desk has more free space than cluttered space. Think of the ideal ratio as 80% free space and 20% used space (remember the kitchen surfaces?) Mmm, what is your current desk ratio?
- At most, your desk has the following:
    1. computer/laptop
    2. phone/fax
    3. printer (this could also be next to your desk to allow for additional space)

4. diary or desk calendar
  5. stationery holder
  6. personal items
  7. an in- and out-tray system for processing current paperwork.
- Depending on your personal needs, you may need different trays but at least consider having three or four different trays:
  1. 'Immediate action'
  2. 'To pay'
  3. 'To file'
  4. 'To read'
- Open mail regularly, tossing out the envelopes and junk mail immediately, and then placing each piece of correspondence paper in the appropriate tray, thus handling each just *once*. Everything else should be filed (we will get to this tomorrow) or stored.
- Okay, now let's get cracking …
  1. Clear your desk of *everything* right now. Everything.
  2. Clean your desk.
  3. Decide what lifts your energy and is 100% necessary.
  4. Make sure you have about 80% free space.
  5. Create a simple system of trays for your current work.
  6. When you leave your desk at night, remove all the clutter (including coffee mugs) and leave your desk ready to spring into action.
  7. Empty your wastebasket every day.
  8. Enjoy the feeling of knowing you will be greeted by a clear desk.
  9. If you use a bulletin board, take off any unnecessary items so that it is clear and focused, not filled with loads of bits of paper or Post It stickers.

> **TIP:** Place something beautiful on your desk such as flowers, a plant, crystals or anything that evokes your work purpose and inspires you. An inspirational quote or saying on your desk is also great for creating a successful mindset. It is also good to have something personal, such as a family photo.

NOT IDEAL!

Avoid a situation where 80% of your desk is cluttered with food, cups, papers, loads of reminder notes and there is no sense of order. Can anyone else come to your desk and make sense of it if you are out the office and have an emergency work issue?

> **TIP:** Imagine you were suddenly gifted a three-week cruise to the Bahamas and you had to leave in an hour! Is your desk in a state that you could hand it over to someone else before you rush off to catch your boat?

My clients come from all walks of life and corners of the globe. A school/university friend who went over to the UK in 1993 called out for help nearly 20 years later, and this is what he had to say:

I hadn't thrown away much in 20 years and on the back of a recent divorce, a demanding job and making time for my two beautiful children, filing and organizing just hadn't been top of my list of things to do. It had reached the point where actually starting it was the hardest part, but I knew it needed doing as there were important legal documents and expense claims buried in amongst 20 years of paperwork and no filing system worth mentioning. So I flew Kate over (after all, there was literally over £50 000 worth of paperwork to find) and the job commenced. A relentless four days with little sleep and a bonfire of epic proportions later, my house was processed from end to end and sanctuary was restored. Kate is one tough taskmistress but celebrates too when the job is done. Paperwork dispatched, money banked and wine drunk as we watched the excess clutter go up in flames.

'John'

Seeing the burden lifted from those shoulders was something I will cherish forever. I went back again to visit him a year later and the sanctuary needed a few nips and tucks (no more than a four-hour top up) but was largely in tact …

Day 17 - Office or study (Part 2)

After tackling your desk yesterday, I trust that there is a hint of excitement as the possibility of handling some dreaded paperwork and getting it sorted looms closer? While some people find paperwork impossible, others merely difficult and a few souls even easy and energizing, I have yet to come across anyone who *loves* doing their own paperwork. It is just one of those tasks that, on completion, will give you a feeling of relief and a sense of order, but very seldom elicits unmitigated joy …

My angle when it comes to your filing is to focus on the benefit of having it all up to date. Knowing you will no longer lose even a minute of sleep worrying about where an important document is, nor lose any vital energy stressing about the mess in your filing system, is a great goal to work towards. It is a real treat to have a simple system of filing that mirrors your life and work needs.

Another way of taking it beyond the mundane is applying the rule of Legacy I mentioned earlier: 'If I were to die today, have I left my life in acceptable order for my loved ones to clear up after me?' Even more inspiring is to remember the cruise you won yesterday!

You can complete this – I know you can!

My aim is that, after completing this process once, you will never have to do it to these extremes again. It will become a way of life. You will never again have to commit this level of time and energy, and will be able to keep on top of everything in your life in a healthier and more productive way.

Okay, back to today's task … Yesterday you were required to clear your desk area, and I mentioned that we would be looking at your filing system today, as there were probably documents from your desk that need a proper home. So, let's get to it!

> **FACT:** The average US executive wastes six weeks per year searching for missing information in messy desks and files. (That translates into one hour per day.) – *The Wall Street Journal*, Esselte study

Filing

'Filing' is the one word that conjures up loads of anxiety in most people. So, whether it is home or office filing, it all amounts to the same thing: how structured and ordered you are in keeping everything in the right place.

If you loathe doing something, chances are it will create havoc in your life and waste hours of your time. For example, if you hate filing and can't be bothered to keep things in the right place and let everything pile up, then complete chaos ensues. Why?

You will spend hours looking for documents, which in turn reinforces how much you hate filing because you now have to wade through shoddy piles of papers – enough to make the hair on your head frizz and the 'overwhelmed' button to hit overdrive!

IDEAL: **IT'S ALL ABOUT RETRIEVAL**
- You are able to retrieve any paperwork within 30 seconds.
- As soon as you hold any piece of paperwork in your paws you know exactly what to do with it immediately. You handle each document only once, by doing one of the following with it:

> 1. You either *throw it out* or *shred* it immediately.
> 2. *File* it away in its proper 'home' for future reference and retrieval.
> 3. *Delegate* it to the relevant person to action.
> 4. Place it in one of your current working piles for you to *action* (one of the in-trays created yesterday).

- Filing is weird in that it includes 'physical' pieces of paper, bills, forms and policies, for example, but – due to the nature of it – can also be considered 'energetic' clutter. So much of what the paper represents to us goes beyond what we see before us. So when your filing is up to date, not only will it physically affect your space more positively, but it will also make you feel more in tune with yourself, prouder, more organized, more up to date and thus more committed to excellence.
- Remember that when you are filing you are doing so for one reason only:

Easy retrieval!

- There are a couple of ways to file all your paperwork, so you need to pick one that works for you. This should correspond with how you are naturally inclined to sort through things in your head when you think about them. What is the first way you would describe your car, for example? When you think about your car, do you think 'motor vehicle', 'transport' or 'Jeep'? And how would you file it for retrieval? The three most common filing methods are:
    1. Alphabetically
        – A could include *Air-conditioner manual* and *AA membership*
        – B could include *Beth's school reports* and *Birth certificate*
        – C could include *Contracts* and *Cell-phone statements*
        – T could include *Tax* and *Telephone bills*
    2. According to broad categories specific to the different aspects or areas of your life, for example: *Travel, Insurance, Cars, Guarantees, Home loan, Banking, Kids*.
    3. According to a color code: green for *Garden*, blue for *Home*, red for *Work*.
- Whichever filing method you choose, you may want to keep an index sheet that reminds you where everything is filed just until you get used to it all.

> **TIP:** You could focus on setting up your system today, and choose to spend tomorrow allocating all your filing into the right area.

- The first layer of filing is to gather all like pieces together so that everything in one category is finally together. Follow these easy steps:
    – **Step 1**: Collect all the bits of paper from around the house, empty the cupboard where most documents are kept and work in an area with lots of floor space.
    – **Step 2:** Clean the cupboards from which you retrieved most of the documents.
    – **Step 3:** Have pen and paper at hand to list the categories.
    – **Step 4:** Pick up one document at a time and decide what category it would fall under by thinking about how you would retrieve it when you need it.
    – **Step 5:** Write the title of that category on scrap paper, and start a section on the floor for all other bits of paper that will fall under that category.
    – **Step 6:** Continue with each piece of paper, one by one.
    – **Step 7:** Throw trash and irrelevant paperwork out as you go.
    – **Step 8:** You will end up with several piles (or 'categories') that can now be filed appropriately.

- I am often asked, 'Where is the best place to store all my filing?' The choices are typically as follows:
    1. a simple concertina-type file bought at any office supply store if you do not have too much paperwork
    2. lever-arch files
    3. good old-fashioned metal filing cabinets with hanging files
    4. stacked stationery holders with drawers (bought ones typically have about six drawers)
    5. a plastic file box with hanging folders and paper filing sleeves (available from any office supply store)

> **TIP:** Generally, I do not recommend using cardboard boxes for your filing system. Boxes stacked with paper stored horizontally rather than vertically make it more difficult to retrieve documents because you have to wade through the entire contents to find something at the bottom of the pile! Boxes are great for archiving old paperwork though!

NOT IDEAL!

- Your filing is months or even years out of date and you have piles of accumulated documents that are all cluttered together, and you have no idea what is where. If you were to look for something it would take you ages to figure out where to start looking, let alone actually locate the information you need.
- Having business and personal papers mixed up together creates havoc.

> **TIP:** Parkinson's Law tells us that: 'A task swells in perceived complexity and enormity in direct relation to the time allotted for its completion.' So just do it! Don't think that because we are dedicating two days to filing, you will leave it for tomorrow to do it enthusiastically. You will need to allocate your full two hours anyway, because this is usually a big task for everyone. Give yourself time by spreading it out over two days to get on top of it and make a big dent.

Day 18 - Office or study (Part 3)

Welcome to Day 2 of sorting out your filing system. Are you pulling your hair out or are you feeling fabulous? Maybe a bit of both? Paperwork requires persistence so keep at it today. Try the recommended addition of music or a friend to keep you on track. Also, working at a bit of speed can help – decide within three seconds where the document needs to go and keep moving so you get through it all as fast as possible. No dithering, just decisions.

Scrunching up the ones to toss out can add to your energy. Heck, you can even try to have fun while doing it – remember what it is that you wish to manifest. You can even take the expanding pile of trash and recycle it, or it might be better for you to burn if it some of the paper work is highly emotional and carries old energy for you – find a way to transmute it.

Getting rid of old documents and ordering the ones you are storing is a powerful sign to the universe that you are creating good space for more opportunities and adventures to come your way, because you will have freed up time and energy to do other things now.

> **TIP:** Filing can be an area that causes unspeakable stress and anxiety. If so, it may be useful to call in someone to help – an organised friend, colleague or a professional like myself to get 100% on top of this.

So often clients find money, policies, forgotten treasured items when finally addressing the clutter that is their non-existent filing system.

Do you remember Craig, who found a policy he had forgotten about? You can find all sorts of interesting things when clearing out your paperwork. What did *you* find?

Wow. It's all coming together! I am so chuffed with how the ol' homestead is looking. If you all know how undomesticated I am you will know what a feat this is. I have passed up social time, which has always been big in my world, to get a good uncluttering in.

Even my office looks awesome. The deal with myself is that it comes in, gets handled and goes out the same day and if it has to stay it has a home in a basket, but can't be there at the end of the week. E-mails are nicely controlled with an archive and rules – all 14 000 of them :)

Marlene

Day 19 – Body and car

Phew! Filing! Having your documented life in order is one of the most exhilarating feelings, flooding your body with relief and order. We are down to the last few days for tackling the physical side of clutter, and are about to spend the last seven days dealing with all the energetic clutter. So give it all you've got and just *go for it!*

Your body

When it comes to your physiological body clutter, I have eased up on you a little this week, so it's time to take another look at that aspect. Today I want you to think about a great reward for all the actions you have been taking since we started because it's time to treat yourself.

Today I would like you to book yourself some form of detoxification treatment with a professional. You may have already done this if you were battling along alone, because I suggested this already, but even so, today is all about reward. You are being put on notice to rise to this challenge today. It doesn't matter what you choose to do, but rather that you choose something that will assist your body. Ideally, book it for within the next week. Think aroma-detox, body wrap or a massage, for example.

And, if you are already coming up with excuses as to why you can't do this, then you need to find a productive way to deal with them, and simply get yourself pampered with a purpose! Some common excuses you may be thinking right now:

- **I don't have the time.** Well, I would counter your argument by suggesting that if you make the time to look after yourself and help your body to help itself, you will be rewarded with clearer energy,

better sleep, more creativity, much-needed downtime, as well as self-esteem and a body that feels so much better. And all of that will instantly translate into greater productivity.
- **I don't have the spare cash right now.** Then get creative with your bartering skills. We all have gifts and talents, so find someone willing to swap their time and ability for something you can offer in return – a great way to do business every now and then. I have used this to great effect to experience something I might not have been able to when cash flow was tight. Or perhaps it's time to take all the things you are letting go of down to one of the buy-and-sell outlets and sell them to convert them to a special treat?
- **I don't know where to go.** Really? Ask a friend, browse the Internet or ask your local health shop for a recommendation. Everyone knows someone …

The bottom line is to find somewhere to go and have a professional treatment that will help your body throw off toxins. You could choose something from the following list:

- **Aromatherapy:** This works on the lymphatic system and assists with drainage. Specifically ask that the aromatherapist use detoxifying oils.
- **Reflexology:** This stimulates your body's reflexes to help in the healing and detox process.
- **Specialized body wrap:** There are a few different wraps that either rebalance your body's minerals, detox your organs or shift your lymph fluid, for example. Ask for the best one for your needs.
- **Body scrub followed by a massage:** The scrub will rid your skin of toxins (just like you have been doing at home), but it's easier when someone else does it. Follow this with a massage to get everything shifting.
- **Spa day:** Go for gold and book a half-day at the spa with a few all-in-one treats designed to get toxins shifting from your body.
- **Colonic irrigation:** If you're up for it, you could book in for some colonic irrigation. Definitely not for the faint-hearted but great for a deep-body and intestinal/bowel clear-out. Not exactly what I would have on my pamper list, but it could be just what the doctor ordered. However, be sure that you go to someone who is highly qualified!

As soon as you have booked your treat or reward, it is time to get to today's actual clutter task.

Your car

Today you need to clean out your car. Your car is an extension of you and your personality, and reflects what you feel about yourself as you go about engaging in your life.

IDEAL: BE PROUD

- Anyone can get into your car right now and you will be proud. Your car is clear from clutter and has just a few essential items that make traveling easier. It is regularly cleaned on the inside and outside. It also smells great.
- Make sure that your spare tire is in good condition and pumped up and that you have the right tools and even a flashlight in the trunk in case of emergencies. These little actions also form part of being up to date with your life at all levels.

> **TIP:** If you do not own a car, then tend to your own form of transport – your motorcycle, bicycle, or even your boat. Alternatively, simply go back to one of the tasks we have already covered. You know which areas need more attention …

NOT IDEAL!

- Your car houses your entire office, all your old food wrappers, used water bottles and the aftermath of two months' worth of gym workouts. Your car is your mobile trash can! Always have a plastic bag for trash, especially if you have loads of passengers, and clear it out at least every second day.
- Your car is packed with equipment that you don't need. If you are one of those people who genuinely need to travel with lots or sports equipment or gear for work, for example, then create compartments in your trunk. Open-topped, collapsible crates work wonders to stop things moving all over the car, thus preventing clutter havoc. You can also get great car-seat hangers that go behind the front seats to organize traveling goodies such as kids' things, wet wipes, a flashlight and maps, for example.
- You have forgotten that your car or bike is an extension of you, one that gifts you the ability to get out and about, do business and get to play with the people you love. Treat it with respect and value it as you do yourself.

Day 20 – Your choice!

Let's take a quick look back over the past 19 days to see what you have already accomplished. I trust you have been documenting your journey along the way with fabulous Before, During and After photos. If you have, then please share some on the community website – you could be our next winner of awesome prizes if yours are chosen as the best clear-up from *Live light, live large!*

Here is a list to remind you, and boost your energy so that you can give today and tomorrow a last blast for good measure. We have covered the following in daily order:

- Bedroom (including your nightstand and under your bed)
- Bathroom (including your cabinets and storage)
- Purse or wallet and handbag or briefcase
- Wardrobe (including shoes, and clothing both shelved and hanging)
- Detox
- Kitchen (including cupboards, fridge and freezer)
- Dishes, cutlery and appliances
- Books and magazines
- CDs
- Photographs
- Living space
- Dining room
- Desk
- Filing
- Car

And here we are today! Isn't it great to look back and see what shifts you have made in less than three weeks? As you plan for today, always remember the basics of your five boxes, and how to go about clearing an area from start to finish – I bet it is forever etched in your psyche. Most importantly, whenever you are letting go of something that no longer serves you, remember to work with your mindful intention so that you make space for something more meaningful to show up in your life.

> Today I am letting go of XYZ, which no longer serve me, in order to make space for _____.

I would like you to spend time today in one of the other areas that have probably been gathering clutter for ages. But I'm going to give you a few options because we all live in different spaces and different-sized homes, so one may be more appropriate for you than the other. Remember that at the end of the course, you may need to redo or complete several areas if you had oodles of clutter to start with. Pick one of the following areas to concentrate on today:

- **Kids' rooms:** If you have children and they have not automatically cottoned on and cleared out their rooms (or if they are too young), get cracking in one of those.
- **Spare room:** If you have a spare room that has been driving you nuts, go for this space!
- **Linen closet:** You could focus on your linen and towels that need clutter clearing – as well as everything else that may have found its way into the linen closet.
- **Trunks and chests:** These inevitably start to overflow as the members of the household consider it an all-purpose storage facility for the day-to-day use of everyone in the home. They're not. They need to serve a purpose.
- **TV/playroom:** If you don't already have one, then it's probably on your wish list. But these multi-purpose rooms are generally the first to succumb to the Dumping Ground Syndrome.

Because we have been concentrating our attention on the better-used living spaces in your home, these last few areas can be quite a big task to tackle. So pick an area you can zap today!

> **TIP:** Remember to keep the main function of the room top of mind and do not confuse the spaces.

Kids' rooms

Usually from the age of three and older, kids can start being co-responsible for their space. Teach them to respect their space from a young age, and lay some ground rules for tidying up, whether once a week or every day. Every time you do it *for* them, you're failing them by not teaching them rules, boundaries or how to look after and respect their belongings.

Teach your children the 'One in, one out' rule with toys, and use particular times of the year to clear out – holidays, birthdays and Christmas, for example – to make space for new or age-appropriate toys.

If you have or are planning to have more children, you may well fall into the fairly common trap of wanting to keep it all for the younger child. When clothes or toys are no longer appropriate for the older child, box them up and mark them properly and remove them to another storage area (such as the spare room or the garage).

The spare room

Ideally, the spare room should always be ready to receive guests; these rooms should have hanging and shelf space for guests' belongings; the bedside tables are completely empty; and the cupboard space is neatly packed. You want guests to feel welcome and not as if they've been relegated to the junk room. The aim is a homely bed-and-breakfast feeling!

Charmayne shares her story – her second bedroom had become a kind of shrine to her deceased sister, and we needed to gift her release from that painful chapter so she could embrace the present and create a beautiful guest bedroom.

> Before Kate came into my life and home to help me de-clutter, I had been nursing my elder sister, Mercia, who was suffering from breast cancer that was rapidly spreading. After my sister passed away, I cluttered her room and was unable to bring myself to go into the room and sit there remembering the wonderful times we had shared together. I was a wreck to say the least, and was missing her so badly that anything that belonged to her was everywhere in heaps in the wardrobe.
>
> Upon Kate's visit to help me de-clutter, the long-awaited emotions came toppling out after years of being pent up. Once we started on Mercia's room, I felt a heaviness lift from me, as I had to finally put my sister to rest and tidy the room to the original lovely room she had turned it into.

Needless to say, I have to thank Kate for allowing me my emotions, as we shared what I could keep and what I needed to de-clutter.

It is now a year and a half later and the room is still neat and tidy. I received visitors from Australia last year, so I was so thankful that I had met Kate. They loved the room as I had changed the bed into a different position, but still had all the beautiful linen and cushions my sister had bought. They were totally relaxed and slept well.

I am still convinced that every time I lie on her bed, [my sister] is smiling at me and I remember her as the whole person she was before she became ill. I will never forget her.

Thank you, Kate, you are awesome.
Charmayne

Linen closet

As a rule, each bed in your home ideally needs three sets of linen: one on the bed, one in the wash cycle and one for spare just in case. You can either store your entire home's linen in one common space – a passage or hall closet, for example – or you can keep each room's linen in that room. Choose whichever option makes sense to you and your space.

If you choose to keep all your linen in one place, you need to decide how you would like to store it for easy retrieval:

- Like with like: all pillowcases together, double sheets together, duvet covers in different sizes, for example – and then label the shelves so that everyone knows what belongs where
- Room by room: each room's linen together in one place, labeled with the owner's name
- Set by set: one whole set together for each bed, complete with sheets, pillowcases and duvet covers in one pile, with spares in their own piles.

The TV/playroom

These rooms are usually common-space areas and require vigilance so that everyone knows the rules of the place. Make sure that you have enough storage to make the space easy on the eye, and to make tidying up a cinch. Install extra shelves, and CD or DVD racks as needed. Use bookshelves and magazine holders to contain objects in their rightful space. Chests and trunks are great for toys. Keep remotes, cables, plugs neatly stored so that the space is safe and user friendly.

We called in Kate and her team because my house was disorganized and family and staff alike had no idea where to begin to keep it tidy. It was sapping energy from all the people in the home. Halfway through the process I felt excited and ready for the change. By the end – exhausted, but happy that everything was ordered. Now – everything seems a little clinical (but that is in the face of utter chaos before). I am now re-evaluating where things should logically be for me. Still happy! I would rate the overall experience as a 9 out of 10 with all ideas given being very useful. The service was incredible and the follow-through with disposing of donation goods and sold items was incredible. I have already sewed my daughter an apron from our 'stash' of material and have promised to make a dress! I am keeping things neat. I love knowing where everything is and that my children are taking responsibility for their playroom!

I am now noticing all the things on the outside of the house that need fixing ... Watch this space! The hardest part for me will be keeping stuff in the right place. The easiest part was clearing out the stuff I didn't need.

Kate arrived on time with her team of people and explained the process to us. Then engaging with everyone in the home – family and staff – she began. I decided to start with the hardest space – my bedroom, as I am the worst (if not the oldest) clutterer in our home. It took hours to do that space. Lunch was a welcome break and already I could start to see the changes. The end of the day was greeted with a dozen or more bags of goods to be donated sitting in the middle of my home. My husband and I were tired but ready for another day.

Day 2 began with more focus as we still had a lot to achieve in a single day. We achieved a lot and at the end of the process identified some things that could be sold (almost a third of the fee was paid back by goodies sold). We are all looking forward to inviting Kate for tea to show off improvements we've made and to show off our tidy home ... also to feed her some yummy cake that I will make with my newly tidied and neatened cake-decorating goodies! I am nervous about being able to maintain the systems put into place, but resolve to not let the house get out of hand ever again. Overall, we had a great experience. Our children love being part of it and our staff loves the control they have over space. Kate is incredibly intuitive and efficient.

AMJ

Now, as a heads up for tomorrow, I am suggesting you rally around and get some help or hire labor to work in one the following areas, which are real toughies to conquer. You may even want to postpone this last task to a weekend and dedicate a little more time and muscle power to zap it totally!

- Garden shed
- Work shed
- Garage
- Basement
- Storeroom or off-site storage
- Attic

These are often spots where we hide many layers and collective years of clutter, because we don't generally see or look at these spaces very often. They're easy to simply ignore for long periods.

You may need to take bite-sized chunks for these last few areas as they are often too large to tackle on their own, or need additional muscle power.

Day 21 - That big area

So let's give it one final shot to get your last big task done and dusted.

Which of the areas have you decided to throw your energy into? Most of these big spaces harbor the really old stuff that has been lurking there forever, so you need to pull on your 'big girl panties' – boys too – and do what needs to be done.

Stay as focused as possible, using the energy created from the past clutter-clearing weeks to support these bigger areas.

> **TIP:** After you have cleared out and know how much stuff you have left to organize, consider installing additional shelves, cupboards and hooks so that you are not left with piles on the floor. If you are keeping lots of stuff, ensure that it is all labeled, like with like, stored properly and easily accessible for when you need them.
>
> Containerize using small and large plastic tubs, cabinets and storage drawers to capitalize on space. Allow these larger areas to reflect the rest of your home.

Home storage

Align your entire home to reflect the new, clutter-free you. Be ruthless, ruthless, ruthless! Keep only what you need and will use – and be three times as strict in big areas such as the garage, storeroom and attic because it is here that we tend to have more space at our disposal to keep stuff 'just in case' …

These spaces typically have old items bought but never used, piles of wood for one day never, and lots of bigger items to throw out, which is why I suggest that you call in additional help.

Focus on the end result, with the aim of clearing every last nook and cranny. Apply everything you have learned and implemented over the past three weeks to zap this area. Use every ounce of insight, knowledge and skill and apply it in super clutter-clearing form.

Off-site self-storage units

I am a huge fan of off-site storage, but only if it means that you are able to keep your office and home environment 100% clutter free. Many people choose to expand beyond the reasonable seams of their home and take additional off-site storage. Just look at these statistics …

> **FACT:** There are now over 48,500 primary self storage facilities in the United States as of year-end 2014; another 4,000 are secondary facilities ('primary' means that self storage is the primary source of business revenue). – US Census Bureau; SSA

IDEAL: STORING OFF SITE
Off-site facilities are ideal for the following situations:

- Keeping excess filing need for tax purposes, for example
- Furniture and household goods if you are relocating and are renting for a while and not yet sure what to do with bigger items
- If you are taking an extended trip and renting out your home and wish to get some precious items out the way.

The SSA (Self Storage Association) states that the self storage industry in the United States generated $27.2 Billion in annual U.S. revenues (2014). The industry has been the fastest growing segment of the commercial real estate industry over the last 40 years and has been considered by Wall Street analysts to be "recession resistant" based on its performance since the economic recession of September, 2008. – www.selfstorage.org

NOT IDEAL!

Whatever your reason for needing self-storage, you would do well to implement a cut-off point on their use. It is not an ideal situation if the space:

- simply becomes a lazy extension of not making decisions
- is little more than a 'dump-all' of procrastination
- allows you to con yourself in some way
- means that you can simply extend the agreement and continue to ignore your stuff.

But out of sight is out of mind. Recent statistics show that people are leaving their junk in storage units for longer and longer. Data from the UK SSA suggests that the average length of stay has risen from 22 weeks in 2007 to 38 weeks in 2010.

The SSA says tenants stay longer than they assume they will rent. Storage properties experience a regular turnover rate, but most tenants stay for long periods – and some tenants never leave!

For example, one client – Georgie – had been storing her excess stuff in an off-site garage and paying for it every month. When we spent just four hours sifting through it, she was able to finally face it all.

She had spent a total of $1,000 storing her household items; in the end she sold 80% of them for only $555 (a total loss amounting to $445). However, if she had sold them at the very beginning she would have made $555 plus saved $1,000 on storage fees! That's a vacation valued at $1,555, right there!

She gave 15% of her stuff to charity and kept a mere 5% of her total goods.

It's been over six months since Kate assisted me with clearing my storage garage before I sold everything. Clearing the household items with Kate holding my hand was a blessing. Her kind and caring manner of highlighting each and every item before 'placing' it made it easier to release the item. I now feel completely free of stuff that was stored for 18 months that really didn't serve me. And I made some money from it too.

Georgie Colling

Day 22 – Shifting to emotional clutter

It is the last week of the program and finally time to switch gears to the emotional baggage. You are ready to address this, because all that you have been doing up until now has been paving the way to tackling your emotional clutter.

> I had the need for moving on with my life and clearing out all emotional barriers sealed by the clutter all around my home, inside my home and especially my office space. I felt anxious, scared and excited all at the same time [but] also a bit uncertain before we started. Halfway through I was tired, relieved and motivated and not to forget the extreme excitement. By the end I was emotional, thankful and **so** happy to see all of my space and the beauty of it; for the first time in the last two years I really want to be in my own space and company. Lots of painful emotions lifted [because] the clutter is not there to sidetrack me any longer. [It] feels spacious, clean and inviting. I have realized that the way I treat my surroundings is a mirror of the way I think ... the right mindset will attribute towards positively moving forward with living my life in a rewarding way. The hardest part was dealing with the finality of closing the book on the past and opening a new book called **My Future** – scary and liberating as well. The easiest part was following the method Kate uses – and throwing all the excess on the 'to go' pile – [and] not having to deal with handling things more than once. Maintaining the systems put in place seems possible with the least bit of effort and daily maintenance – above all practice discipline learned through the clutter coaching of Kate. I rate her service 10/10.
>
> *Manda*
> Tsitsikamma

Regardless of whether you have managed to commit to your daily hour or not, the fact is that by simply being willing and participating in this program, you have taken more steps than most. I bet that something emotional has already shifted in your life at some level?

I would love to hear your stories, and how letting go has made way for new things to come your way. With more space in your home or office, better organization, and a newfound mindfulness of your body and its needs, I think you are ready for embarking on the last leg of this journey.

Once again, I want to remind you that you can e-mail me at marketing@kate-emmerson.com for help or encouragement – with all the emotional and energetic clutter being looked at, you may welcome a little extra support.

Back to the boxes

If for any reason you did not clear out all five boxes you were left with yesterday, then make some time today, or at least by the end of this week, so that the huge task of clearing your physical clutter is up to date and complete by Day 28. Do whatever is necessary to get up to speed.

> **TIP:** Go back and take a look at the clutter assessment you did on Day 2, just to familiarise yourself with your original answers and remind yourself of the areas that challenge you emotionally.

Energetic clutter

You are now going to shift your attention to the final area of clutter in order to let go of other 'stuff' that may be clogging up your life in a different way. This category of clutter is one of the hardest to deal with, because it means unpacking – in the broadest sense – the deep, personal baggage we hold on to. It is invisible and nebulous and thus harder to locate: we can't really see it; we can only really feel its energy and see the negative effects.

This type of clutter covers everything that takes up emotional, mental and spiritual space in your life. If you have loads of energetic clutter, or baggage in some shape or form, you will find that your life is stagnant and dull, and you are not very happy. This is because you have not been able to let go at the appropriate time, and still lurking in your subconscious is a series of negative emotions: anger, resentment, guilt, betrayal, hurt, disappointment, a lack of boundaries, bad communication, shoddy time management, a lack of real honesty and a reluctance to speak up when you want to.

There may be loads of unresolved issues that make you feel 'used' and taken advantage of. Sound familiar? This is the clutter that clogs up your ability to get on with life and to feel a sense of deep inner peace and freedom to be yourself. It will sabotage your ability to engage freely with others in a healthy, adult manner. In short, energetic clutter creates *havoc* and causes *chaos*. This could even lead you into certain types of non-productive relationships and engage in communication that does not serve you in some way. Emotional clutter will stop you from taking pride in yourself, developing self-respect and making yourself a priority. You will find that you are controlled and always look to please other people, or take things personally.

This clutter requires a different perspective if you want to bring your life more up to date and free your energy. I find that those clients who consistently negotiate their true values, look for recognition from everyone but themselves. They are always too scared to stand up for themselves and speak their truth. These are the individuals who experience the negative impact of energetic clutter.

So start thinking very specifically about what could be going on in your life right now that would fall under 'energetic clutter'. Remember that clutter is anything that no longer serves you in some way and is no longer adding value to your life. What matters is that you are able to be honest and start recognizing what no longer serves you.

What's tripping you up?

It's time to let go of some of the issues that are holding you back. Consider some of the following reasons:

- Unfinished relationships
- Unresolved issues (the ones that leave a knot in your tummy!)
- Broken agreements
- Unfulfilled promises
- Rumors that require your action to stop them
- Money owed to you
- Financial debt
- Favors owed to you and by you
- Unanswered letters, e-mails and messages
- Not being honest about who you are

- Friends and acquaintances who do not add value to your life
- Attitudes that bog you down and prevent you from moving forward
- Habits, such as bad time management or poor self-talk
- Self-limiting beliefs
- The 'To do' list lurking in the mental plane
- Negotiated commitments (such as exercising or giving up smoking)

All of the above prevent a real sense of emotional, mental and spiritual harmony, which can in turn lead to disorder or even disease. Can you identify some areas in your life right now that could do with some serious clutter clearing to give you a fresh burst of energy? When you take care of the emotional, less visible aspects of your life you will find that you suddenly have an abundance of 'bounce' and improved self-esteem too. You are able to release untold amounts of energy that you can utilize in the here and now. Clearing emotional clutter will also release feelings of stagnation and frustration and bring your energy levels up to 100%.

So, let's start the emotional baggage journey …

Making appointments

Today is all about getting back up to date with all your appointments. These can relate to any area of your life. When we know that there are things we should be doing, but we never get around to doing them because we're 'too busy', we feel overwhelmed and useless, a total failure.

Make sure you're drinking lots of water while you're tackling this task. It is still important to be maintaining the vital routine you have established over the past three weeks.

IDEAL: MAKING AND KEEPING TIME
- Your life is up to date, with relevant appointments in all aspects of your life in place. Even if you are very busy, you make time for all the important things that keep your life running smoothly, including all your personal appointments.
- When you think of your life, there is no negative self-talk about what you should or ought to be doing.
- You have ample time and space for everything. This sounds relatively simple and fairly easy to achieve, right? Well, it is! But how often do we put off something till tomorrow – and especially if it does not fall under the realm of 'unbelievably urgent'?

- Do you recall the negative implications of clutter – one of them being your reputation? Start taking yourself seriously and acting professionally, with integrity and self-appreciation, and see how the world starts responding to you. One simple way to achieve this is to get everything scheduled in, even if it is only for a month or two down the line.

Think about your life, and anything that springs to mind that requires some action today. Use the rest of your hour to get down and do it. Here are some triggers just in case you need them, and remember to think about the rest of your family too if you're responsible for them (such as children or the elderly):

- Business appointments (especially those you have been avoiding), with staff, your boss, clients, suppliers, Human Resources, lawyers
- Medical appointments with the dentist, doctor and gynae (remember mammogram and prostrate checks, cholesterol, diabetes, blood pressure, for example)
- Car, bike or boat services
- Computer, telephone and other technical support
- Extra lessons and tuition
- Repairs to electrics and plumbing
- Finances (the annual appointment booked with your financial advisor)
- Updated will and insurance
- Social (concert tickets, that picnic you've been wanting to have with friends or simply sitting down to write to and catch up with friends)
- Car license, ID, passport, visas for traveling
- School, varsity or parent-teacher meetings
- Beauty and pampering appointments (hairdresser, nails, facials)
- Renewing or canceling newspaper or magazine subscriptions

NOT IDEAL!

You stagger under the weight of ever-increasing demands and pressures – both real and imagined, from having hundreds of small and large tasks or appointments you know you need to make but never get around to doing.

> **TIP:** For recurring appointments, such as with the dentist or for your hair or car service, it is much easier to make the next appointment before you even step out the door after the previous appointment. That way it's already locked into your calendar and more likely that you fulfill it once already booked. Make a promise that if you have to cancel it, that you rebook it in the same phone call.

Day 23 – Honesty

How does it feel to have made headway into all the things on that dreaded 'One day I'll do them' list? I hope you feel lighter and more positive today from those little action steps you took yesterday.

The courageous emotional conversation

Today I would like you to think about all the individuals you consider 'family and friends' in your life. I especially want you to think about your partner, husband, wife, children, your nuclear family, your larger extended family, your in-laws, housemates and anyone else you feel is part of your inner clan. As you think about each of them, imagine that they are all gathering at your home right now.

As you all come together, think about who you may have unresolved issues with right now. Maybe there is something you need to 'clear' with Aunty Joyce, or call Peter up on that remark he made to you last time. Is there any unfinished business or unsaid words that would make you feel awkward if all your family and friends were together?

Masks

Often when we gather with our family and loved ones we wear masks. Yep, masks! Wearing masks keeps you small …

Working as a life coach and clutter expert, I have to tell you that pretty much every person I work with has issues around self-esteem in some shape or form, and thus ends up wearing some kind of mask in order to like themselves or to get other people to like them. It is part of how we develop and progress as we grow older. We are born in the awesome glory of something bigger than ourselves, yet we embark on a journey as humans that seems to make us forget our inherent magnificence, our true beauty and our purpose.

We get stuck and caught in the trap of life here on earth. This means we often play small and behave like victims in our own lives. We start hiding, cutting off or ignoring aspects of our true self, merely as protection.

What you need to remember is that you can only play small and insignificant with your own permission – no one else can force this upon you. But we like to wear our protective masks, which cover up our true selves, and then blame others for the position we take. In other words, we may play the family clown at family functions in order to keep the peace, and then blame our siblings for not being present emotionally, which is why we feel we have to fill that gap. Or we may feel the need to play the successful one, brave one or the quirky one … It all gets so complicated doesn't it?

When we wear masks of any description, we are not being 100% honest with either ourselves or others. This leads to complex and unhappy relationships where we are not free to be who we are.

Sound at all familiar? What would your life be like right now if you were brave enough to remove some of your masks? Which is the one you hide behind the most, the one that keeps your guard up so beautifully when it comes to relationships? Every masked interaction you have has a deep in-authenticity that ripples from it and negatively affects your emotional and mental body. Although the intention of the mask may be a positive one – to keep you safe or to get people to like you – there is always another way to satisfy this intention in a way that serves you more holistically.

So, brave soul, what is it going to be?

I challenge you to be honest with yourself, to mindfully remove one mask that keeps you stuck at some place in your life when it comes to relationships, and be brave enough to see what happens once you take that step.

Take a moment to examine what you need to do that will in some way solve an unresolved conversation, heal an issue, nurse a hurt or anything else that is getting in the way of an otherwise happy and fulfilling relationship. Then take action on whatever you have decided you need to do by having that courageous conversation, whether in person, over the phone or even by writing a letter.

> *Taking off the mask has been the hardest for me. I smile, walk around all bubbly, like nothing is wrong. I am exceptionally good at masking. Day 23 hit right home for me and was the most effective of all the tasks. In fact, on the day I had to book an appointment I booked a dentist's appointment, but after doing my Day 23, I went and booked for a counseling session too. I made an appointment and will take it from there. This was after writing a letter to my late*

sister (who's daughter I have adopted). I cannot express the feeling; it was emotional, relieving, liberating, sad and happy at the same time.

Then again today I met Lauren and when she asked how the makeover was going, I said all the nice things and deliberately skipped the letter part, because it was uncomfortable for me ... Am I still wearing a mask?

I am learning that this makeover is not just a nice-to-have; it's a life-changing journey based on principles versus events. I am now learning more discipline and honesty [toward] myself, especially about how I feel.

Noni

> **TIP:** You can heal relationships with people who have already passed on by writing a letter to them, and then burning it. The mere act of writing it will help release energy trapped in your body.

Day 24 – Money! Money! Money!

We have just four more days before you complete all 28 days of *Clear Your Clutter* so you can *live light, live large*. Muster up all the energy you can – just to double check if you are still paying attention to your eating, water and generally looking after your vitality.

Finances

This area of life typically causes people a lot of stress. Consider whether any of the following issues are inappropriate for you right now – in other words, not reflecting who you truly are. If for any reason there is anything you need to let go of that is no longer serving you, including a bad habit or pattern of behavior, then today is the day to take steps to sort it out, even if it is just one to get the ball rolling!

Areas that get us into predicaments include:

- Being irresponsible with money in some way
- Using money as a form of control over people
- Never having enough money, always being in debt and behind with payments
- Checks and debit orders bouncing
- Poor management of your money in general
- Being constantly behind with your financial administration
- Old self-sabotaging beliefs about money
- Not providing for your future
- Not taking care of your present
- Money owed to you causing a rift in that relationship
- Money owing to others or the bank
- Behind on all your tax returns
- High interest rates needing to be renegotiated

Money has a lot of emotional energy associated with it. Today you need to spend an hour with your finances in some way that will bring all your energy and attention to the present.

> *I am proud to declare that today all my tasks are now up to date. In actual fact, I did Day 24 on Day 16 because that was the biggest reason I am doing this and it had been bothering me quite a lot! I have now merged my accounts into one and used my savings to pay off my credit card. Hahaha ... I've cleaned up more than just clutter, my bank account is clean too, but then this is the mess of accounts all over and too much interest. I did this with the assistance of a banker and will only see the benefits on my first payday after the initiative, March 2011.*
>
> *Noni*

The above letter is from Noni. Remember her at the start of this book? She has since bought a house …

The essence is to have a healthy relationship with money and how you handle it. Take time today to get energized, take action and feel fabulous that you are more in control again.

All it may take is to sit alone, gather your wits about you and get up to date; or you may need to call your bank manager, a financial coach, do a financial workshop or call about debt review. Perhaps the first step is to have a conversation with your partner to finally tell the truth about where you are at.

You know what to do.

Day 25 – Boundaries

This week remember that you are meant to be having some kind of professional treatment to support your body on its detoxing journey. Helping your body let go will also assist the emotional letting-go you are processing this week. If you didn't manage to book it last week, then make up for this today and give your body a much-needed pampering or detox session. You really do deserve it.

Boundaries and self-respect

Today is all about assessing whether you are consistently negotiating your true values, disrespecting yourself and perhaps looking externally for recognition from everyone but yourself. Are you often scared to stand up for yourself and speak the truth? All too often, we say *Yes* when in actual fact we should be saying *No*. This can be hard to do if you're not used to it, but it is worthwhile in the long run, so do your best. This is about being honest enough with yourself to know what you want, and having the ability and confidence to say what you are feeling inside and sharing that with others. You need to be aligned with what you feel and then ask for it. *I dare you!*

Negotiating boundaries

So how do you know if you are negotiating your boundaries? If you are constantly feeling the following, chances are you are negotiating both yourself and your boundaries:

- You feel you are being taken advantage of.
- You feel used.
- You feel un- or under-appreciated.
- You feel walked all over.
- You feel you are always getting the raw end of the deal.

- You feel grumpy with others because they have what you want.
- You feel resentful and angry, and sulk often.
- You do more for others than vice versa.
- You never have enough time for yourself.
- You are always too busy to do what matters.
- You never stop for a break to refresh yourself.
- You consistently take on too much.
- You always say *Yes*, even if it doesn't suit you.
- You battle to renegotiate commitments.
- You put others' needs ahead of your own, often at your own expense.

This is the big stuff that makes us feel bad, disempowered and play small in our lives.

Do you need to start speaking up, speaking the truth and asking for your needs to be met? The good news is that you can do something about it. All too often we are scared to set clear boundaries as it might mean saying *No* to something or someone, and we may fear that they won't like us any more. Well, the exact opposite happens … As scary as it may seem to have to say *No* for once, when something truly important is asked of your time and energy, people will actually respect you for it when you say *Yes*, because you no longer say Yes as your standard response. It may take some getting used to, and others may even test your resolve, but I can promise you it gets easier, and the rewards are immense.

Consider yourself

Before you offer your habitual response of *Yes* to every request, see if you can automatically tell them you will get back to them with your answer. Then reflect on it, and ask yourself whether you *really* want to do it – and for all the right reasons. Not out of guilt or obligation, which falls into the old trap of fuzzy boundaries. Then do what needs to be done: say *No*. When you start respecting yourself and your boundaries, then others will be able to do the same in return.

> **TIP:** Do not feel that you have to explain why you cannot or will not do something. Great phrases to use are the following:
>
> - I'd love to help you but I'm unable to this time.
> - Thanks for asking, but it really doesn't suit me right now.
> - Let me think about it and I'll get back to you by 5 pm.
> - I'd love to help you but I'm on my own tight deadline. Why don't you do what you can and if by tomorrow morning you are still stuck I can give you 10 minutes (people can usually figure stuff out when given the opportunity …).
> - Let me check my calendar and see if I have capacity for it.

It may be appropriate for you to look at things you have already committed to (for yourself or involving others) that are in fact no longer what you want to do. I suggest that you:

- either find a way to do them as soon as possible to get them out of your space, or
- find the energy and courage to actually *renegotiate* what you said you would do.

I was once commissioned to write for four issues of a magazine, but after three issues it felt really inappropriate for me to continue because I felt my message was not fully aligned with the magazine's target market. As much as the idea of writing for a big magazine publishing 25 000 copies thrilled me, I actually felt the dread getting worse and worse as my deadline loomed nearer. Then I simply decided to pluck up the courage and ask the publisher if I could renegotiate my initial commitment. It was perfect and I was let out of my contract without a blink. And *boy* was I relieved! So, the lesson to be learned here is to get your boundaries clear and take different action today to get a different outcome.

Day 26 – Detox your inbox

It's time to focus on effective productivity. While you could argue that e-mails are physical clutter because they exist on tangible equipment, I feel it is more appropriate to consider them emotional clutter. They are shrouded in obligations, demands and requests and carry a lot of inherent baggage as people feel overwhelmed and controlled by the modern-day dictum that says: *You will be available 24/7 or else!*

The best advice I can offer is to learn to manage your e-mail inbox so that you can spend more quality time on the inbox of your life. Ask yourself: How effective is my current system of handling e-mail? Rate it on a scale of 1–10, with 10 being *Awesome* and 1 being *Overwhelmed* – in other words, your life is being run by your computer, laptop, iPad or Smartphone.

What happens to your energy every time you dare to look at your inbox? Do you dread opening your mail due to the sheer volume of it and what it requires of you? Chances are you feel overwhelmed, irritated or exhausted by always having to be available. Not a great way to be doing business or creating your life from that frame of mind.

Nowadays people live with a common underlying assumption and corresponding guilt trip: feeling immensely pressured to be available and never able to say *No* to the beeping phone or e-mail alert. We all know how integral being 'online' is to our 2013 lifestyles of PCs, laptops, iPhones, iPads, iPods and BlackBerries, which scream at us all day long, demanding our attention. While the freedom of technology catapults us into ever-higher realms of flexibility, it also comes with a profound flip side that requires us to manage it effectively.

We feel that people want us to be available 24/7 and yet, while this can truly stroke our egos and make us feel important, it can also create a real pressure of needing to respond immediately to all requests whether business or personal, serious or silly.

It would be useful to create healthy guidelines and boundaries to understand the benefit of not morphing our online time into every other facet of life. People have generally lost all sense of self as they allow others to control their time, even going so far as being in one meeting while mailing someone via their phone in another meeting. What about the person e-mailing and working in bed when they really would be better off paying attention to their relationship or doing something to expand their sense of self. It is about the fine line between the joy of flexibility versus the consequence of never taking downtime. It even happens when people are in restaurants, eating and talking, yet simultaneously checking Facebook, Twitter, e-mails and the like. You see it all the time …

FACT: The world's capability for storing, communicating and computing information has grown at least 23% annually since 1986. The average person in 2007 was *transmitting the information equivalent of six newspapers each day* and receiving 174 newspapers of data (much of that reflected in video and photos). – Dr Martin Hilbert, *Science Magazine*, February 2011

Think of how much more this is true today. Now *that's* a lot of information to process! We have to manage and be available to our clients, colleagues, boss, friends, family and even kids. Do we really need to take every call from a client? The better we manage our time and our availability, the more effective and simpler our lives will be.

You teach others how to treat you, so if you are always available to the world, that is what they come to expect. So the bottom line is that unless you need to answer emergency calls from your family or are an emergency professional, it's time to get offline.

The following eight-point plan to smarten up your inbox aims to assist you to:

- cut down on actual mail received
- cut down on the number of times you check e-mail
- smarten up your e-mail filing and retrieval system.

1. Set strict rules

Create as many folders for the categories or people to whom and from whom you send and receive mail most often. This gives you a collection point of folders (like the folders for documents on your desktop) that frees up your inbox. You can even set up rules so that certain mails go directly into certain folders, without you even having to drop and drag them manually. Cool!

Play the game that if you were suddenly to take a six-month vacation or land up in hospital, you could direct someone to a specific mail on your behalf in 30 seconds.

2. Remember: Ruthless rocks!

From now on you need to be committed and ruthless in assessing *every single* e-mail you receive – be it from the boss, a colleague, friends, family or the dreaded newsletters you may be subscribed to. Do not simply delete an e-mail thinking you're done.

If you habitually do not read a newsletter within 24 hours of receiving it, the ideal rule is to unsubscribe. Finished. If this thought of potentially missing out terrifies you, at least put every single newsletter you receive into an automatic subfolder; that way you can read them over in your leisure time. If you are not reading them monthly, it's definitely time to unsubscribe and stop conning yourself.

3. Train your colleagues

Teach people that you do not need to be copied in on every single e-mail; if a mail is going to go back and forth more than twice, use the phone to respond; do not reply to every single mail if it is rhetoric. Each e-mail you send is using your precious time and energy, so make sure it counts and is adding value.

> **FACT:** Organizations lose around $1 250 per user in annual productivity because of time spent dealing with spam, $1 800 unnecessary e-mails from co-workers, and $2 100–$4 100 due to poorly written communications. – Tom Pisello, *ITBusinessEdge.com*, December 2008

4. Warn your friends

Politely ask friends not to clog up your inbox with junk – they are free to use your other social media networks for social stuff. That way when they do send you something you know it is of real value.

5. Deal with junk mail

This can be one of the main reasons for a demanding inbox. Most people simply delete the mail with a *tut tut* under their breath, and while your response may deal with *that* mail, it does not solve the ongoing problem. Improve your junk filter, your spam blocks and your online security, and take two seconds to add them to your blocked senders so that there will be a chain reaction to reducing your inbox going forward.

6. Batch your mail

Whilst users of smart devices such as iPhones and Androids might be up in arms at this suggestion, you need to know the productivity law: every time you start one task and then switch to another, you waste time. It is much smarter to let go of the need for instant gratification and get into the effective habit of batching. Spend 20 minutes to an hour of focused time on your e-mail at one sitting rather then being at the beck and call of your inbox every time it beeps. Learn to stay focused on one task. You will process e-mails much faster by batching it into sessions. Trust me on this.

> **FACT:** In 2007, a group of Microsoft workers took, on average, 15 minutes to return to serious mental tasks, such as writing reports or computer code, after dealing with incoming e-mail. They wandered off to reply to other messages or browse the Web.
> – *The New York Times*, 25 March 2007

7. Power processing

Process your e-mail more effectively by sitting down and looking at them. This means that you do not scan your mailbox looking for the ones to respond to, you process them all immediately. What does this look like from a practical point of view?

Well, it means that you deal with it *once*. If you can deal with an e-mail start to finish in less than 30 seconds, just do it. Leaving it to read again and then respond later just takes more time.

8. Finish first

Complete the important task you're busy with before randomly checking your e-mail – this single change in behavior will allow you to do more important tasks first thing in the morning rather than getting lost in masses of e-mails. Spend at least the first hour of your workday on your most vital task, then check your e-mail all at once at, say, 10 am. Tim Ferriss, author of *The 4-hour Work Week*, advocates checking e-mail at 12 noon and then again at 4 pm. This enables most of your previous mail to have been answered and allows you to batch your time the most effectively. If this seems impossible for you, at least stick to the 'no mail for the first hour' rule, and keep batching as often as you can.

When you learn to control your inbox, you instantly become more effective in all areas of life.

> **FACT:** People who regularly juggle several streams of electronic information do not pay attention, control their memories, or switch from one task to another as well as those who prefer to focus on one thing at a time. Heavy media multitaskers are paying a big price.
> – Clifford Nass, Eyal Ophir and Anthony Wagner, *Stanford Report*, 24 August 2009

Day 27 – Forgiveness

'Resentment is like drinking poison and then hoping it will kill your enemies.' – Nelson Mandela

I have often discussed letting go of things that no longer serve us, and taking this to the deeper emotional and energetic level. Today I want to deal specifically with the art of letting go.

Emotional clutter is typically the hardest to clear away, because what manifests externally in your physical environment is only a symptom of the inner world you live with. When we hold onto things from the past that are negative for us, they are like a heavy weight around us, dragging us down at every level. But because these hurts and anger are internal, all too often we are not conscious of the negative effects or even feel the real weight of carrying them around with us. We just live with it.

We bear the negative consequences, but are just too attached or blindsided to let it all go. We sometimes also feel so vindicated in our point of view when we have been wronged that it can be quite rewarding – in its own warped way – to be angry with someone, blame them for something, keep them at a distance to punish them, feel that intense anger, resentment or desire for revenge. We can feel quite self-righteous and smug about it: 'They did this to me!' It can even make us feel good and give us something on which to focus our negative attention.

But what is the real cost for *you* in the end?

You could be using the same amount of energy differently and redirecting it towards something positive, such as a life's dream or goals waiting patiently for you to step up and claim them. But the longer you hold onto past hurts, the less likely it will be that you reach the level of control and success that you say you desire. Perhaps it is finally time to face some of this stuff and shift it. That way you can give yourself permission to come back to being fully present in your life, freeing up your creativity and filling the space in your heart so that you are able to move on to the things that really matter.

Di writes the following after explaining her years of abuse …

> The antidepressant did more harm than good. I became suicidal. I did the landscaping job and then sat with nothing to do, in desperation and suicidal. No work and no one who was willing to help me in any way. I would wake up in the morning and watch TV.
>
> One day I was watching SABC 3's Noeleen on 3 Talk and she said there's a life coach, Kate Emmerson, who is giving away a life-coaching course to someone who has clutter in their life. I had immense clutter in my head.
>
> She replied to my query and said I will help you.
>
> I did her course. Everything that she told me to do.
>
> I was meeting a friend for lunch on a Saturday and was doing the potato thing at the time. I had a huge pack of potatoes with names carved on them and my friend said, 'Can I hold the pack of potatoes to see how much they weigh?' I let her. They all spilled out of the packet on the parking lot. I said we have to retrieve them as I still have another

week to go! And I spent a lot of time carving the names on these potatoes.

We retrieved all but one. It is probably still there, rotting with a person's name carved on it. (This is how Di did her forgiveness exercise by writing letters and having conversations with all the names on potatoes she needed to forgive. Kate)

I would not have survived if not for Kate. She turned my life around. Made me look at life from a different perspective, I learned and listened to what is going on. How to interpret it and how to live with it. And how to handle it. I was a suicidal maniac ready to take my own life to no consequences, **seriously**. I had the noose tied to a pole above a beam and a plan to call the ambulance as I was going to do it!

Never doubt the universe and Kate to get you back on track. She did it for me and I am forever grateful to her for getting me back on track, believing in myself and saying **I can do it**; I am still here because of Kate and her help. Thank you, Kate. You made such a difference in my life and got me back from a useless, suicidal person to a functional, working and happy person.

Life is not always perfect and life cannot always be perfect, but if we can do what we are passionate about and make ourselves happy and make money doing it with integrity and honesty that is all that counts. The rest that we require in life will follow from this. **I am forever grateful.**

Di D

Forgiving and healing

One of the reasons we hold onto this stuff and where we all experience some confusion is that we believe that if or when we forgive someone, we are condoning their actions, reinforcing that what they did or said was okay. And that doesn't feel right because we are genuinely affected by what happened. But forgiveness does *not* mean this at all. When you forgive someone you are not condoning anything they did at *any* level. When you forgive someone else, it really means to give it up for *yourself*, not for them. They need to experience their own healing and find their own forgiveness – that is not your job. Forgiveness is never about the other person, it is about *you*. But when you hold onto the pain, it is only about them and what they did to you. When you are able to somehow, in some way, forgive someone else, what you are really saying is:

> **I am no longer willing to carry around the pain and hurt this has caused me.**

Read that again – it's vital.

In this way, you are responsible for holding onto the past or letting it go. That is your choice. Can you see the difference? Sometimes it can feel near impossible to forgive someone, yet the energy and lightness that you feel afterwards is what will allow you to move forward in leaps and bounds towards that which you set out as your intention at the very beginning of this process.

The truth is you can never understand or even glimpse the real reasons why someone has said or done something to you, and at the end of the day it doesn't matter. What does matter is whether you are still carrying that old energy around.

Can you even begin to imagine what might have happened in South Africa if Nelson Mandela had not been able to forgive everyone and everything that had happened to him and his people? While the country may not be free from all the pain, it has taken incredible steps – some forward, some back, more forward then a few back again … and so it flows.

All behavior has a positive intention if you dig deep enough. Our positive intention when we hold onto fear, hurt and anger, for example, can be to protect ourselves so that it will not happen again or so that we don't trust that person again and thereby be hurt yet again. It can be about survival, keeping our inner child safe, or any number of other personal reasons.

Yet the very nature of holding onto the negative emotions will attract more and more of the same. If you are holding tightly onto that place of pain inside, you may find it hard to see the joy and gifts that are in front of you. The beliefs that you have layered around all the hurt will ensure that you will continue to be at the receiving end of more and more of the same painful experiences. The baggage you carry around weighs you down, like hundreds of those bottles filled with lead.

There comes a time when it becomes vital to your own survival that you let it all go, to forgive in a way that releases *you* from the pain and to finally heal. But for this you have to be willing to let go of what you have been dragging around.

Are you ready to drop your baggage?

> 'None of us can change our yesterdays, but all of us can change our tomorrows.' – Colin Powell, US Secretary of State

This was a very hard, emotional week for me. I cried so much I was exhausted. My eyes looked and felt like bees stung it.

I was able to get to the cause of all the crap I feed myself daily. It all stems from family and cruel kids from the past.

Even though I understand that it is all in the past and I am responsible for my own actions right now, I still let it rule my life. How sad. I use this as an excuse not to get involved in my life. When life gets too hard I give up and enforce my mother's words, 'I am not good enough' or 'I cannot do this.'

So now that we had a great weekend in nature and I wrote a letter of forgiveness and letting go and burned all this, I am so ready to move on. No more excuses or lies.

I am looking forward to shifting all my negatives into positives.

It can only get better from now on; no matter how hard it will be, it will be fantastic.

TJ

> 'A wound not fully felt consumes from the inside.
> We must run very hard if we want to stay one step ahead of this pain.'
> – Oriah Mountain Dreamer

The very best thing you can do today is to look at all the people, attitudes and habits in your life, and take constructive action to *let them go*. One of the best ways to do this is to sit quietly and think carefully about what no longer serves you. It might take you a bit of time, so be patient.

This is about finding all the harsh things that people have done to you that have in some way negatively affected you, dampened your personal fire, or made you angry.

Wander back through your life looking for the following people, and next to their name write the date when the hurtful incident took place or perhaps the age you were when it happened. These people can be dead or alive, in the same country or not. It doesn't matter. You may not even know where they are right now. The simple test is this: If you were somehow to see them today, you would have all sorts of immediate reactions in your head, heart and body. There is unfinished business here. You know what I mean.

1. Look for all those individuals, no matter who they are to you now, or who they were to you then, whom you have never been able to offer 100% *forgiveness*. It doesn't matter what they did, but you know in your heart that you have not been able to forgive them and that you are holding onto that in some way. Write down the date or dates.
2. Next look for all those for whom you feel some kind of *jealousy*, *possessiveness* or *envy*, along with the dates of incidents you can remember.
3. Now look for people who *betrayed* you in some way, and for whom you are still feeling the pain of that betrayal.
4. Next make a list of all the people who said *hurtful* things to you and with whom you have never had the courageous conversation.
5. Make a list of people to whom you need to say goodbye, dead or alive.

Now you need to do some form of letting go – it might be different for each person. You may want to write a letter; you may need to go and visit a grave; you may need to fulfill a promise; you might need to ask to meet – the potential list of how you handle each one is endless. But you will know in your heart what to do for each of the people you have sought out and 'found'.

It is always a great idea with written material of any form to do a kind of ritual to celebrate letting go, through burning what you have written. Go outside and light it, toss it on a fire or use a candle. Then sit quietly and watch all these words you have written be burned away so that you can finally let them go.

Then I suggest you go and wash your hands, take cognizance of the magnitude of the release (it can feel weird for a while, as well as totally liberating) and celebrate in some way at having taken this all-important step.

Hi Kate

I have been asking myself if I should tell you the actual change that came over me with my clutter course. Reason being that if people should find out what feelings I have been walking around with, while on the outside pretending I was happy and content.

Anyway, I told you originally that I bought the house, and did not feel excited about it. I had no will or energy to do anything to the house and in the house.

But during the course, and in doing the visualization techniques, I started getting excited, eager, enjoying doing things. When I moved into the house, I told myself that it means nothing to own a house if I do not have him (my ex-husband) to share it with any more. I was secretly harboring the fact that I wanted him back even after being divorced for five years.

In my notes to you I also wrote about dancing with my grandchildren in my visualization of moving to another house ...

It was at this time that I realized that my visualizations you had taught me to do about my near future no longer included my ex-husband, and I realized that I had let him go.

I now have free will to talk to him and his new wife like they are old friends. In my visualizations, all I saw was a happy **me**!

Radia Berry

Finally every aspect of my home is uncluttered. I am amazed at how easy it has become to chuck the stuff that just isn't adding value – the physical stuff that is – the emotional not so much.

I feel in some ways like an AA member praying, 'Lord, give me the courage to accept the things I cannot change.' I am realizing that even with the best heart and intentions some people will just never reciprocate and I am not going to change things with them – so I have decided to let it go. I am blessed in that I have so many good people who touch my life every day, so I have decided to concentrate on them and am accepting the realization that others have passed through my life to teach me something or so I can have an experience I otherwise wouldn't have.

I can't keep reflecting on what I can do differently and 'what ifs'. It's time to move forward.

Marlene

Day 28 – Setting up systems

I am heaving a sigh of relief with you after all your incredibly hard work. Are you ready to share some of your stories on the online community? Sharing could make the world of difference, and could serve to inspire someone else still needing to get to this part of the journey.

I now want to share some further tips to keep your space clear going forward so that you stay in charge of your life and all your clutter.

Why not start off by relooking at the clutter assessment from Chapter 5 and redoing it now? As you fill it in, notice the vast difference and improvement after all your hard work.

The next steps forward

1. Take a look back at what you were asked to do each day. Evaluate whether you completed an hour or not. If you did not complete the task for whatever reason, then schedule to get 100% up to date with all the tasks this week.
2. Depending on your initial level of clutter, even if you did spend the allotted hours you may not have gotten through it all – and, believe me, this is very common. I know that you might have felt naturally inspired to do more, because this process can be very exhilarating and energizing when you get started, but if for any reason you still have more to do, then why not draw up a brief plan for yourself. What areas you will tackle, and when? These may typically be larger storerooms, the garage, the spare room, the study or even the filing yet *again*.
3. Evaluate how you are doing with that special aspect you wanted to make room for. What have you manifested in line with your intention? Are you finding your intention is flowing more easily towards you and is within reach?
4. Lastly, I would like to share with you a general structure of how to keep your life up to date. Simply tweak it so that it works for you but, above all, put some systems in place for keeping your life clear from now on. It will make such a huge difference to you. Remember that it should ideally take no more than 10 minutes to clear up any room once you have cleared it of clutter. Maintenance will be relatively easy until the next time you need to do a big shift and clear out again. It now only takes you about an hour to clear up your entire house. Remember to keep every member of the household involved and accountable to rules and systems.

Schedule all these little tasks below for the next three months until they become ingrained habits.

Daily

Take a few minutes daily to stay in top form:

- Keep your bedside tables tidy at all times.
- Leave your bedroom as you would like to come home to it.
- Empty your waste basket and dump the contents in the outside trash can at least every second day.
- Always wash dirty dishes and wipe the sink dry afterwards.
- Leave your desk clear in preparation for the next day.
- Manage your inbox carefully and do not let it build up.

Weekly

- Make sure your clothing is put away according to your new system.
- Keep all living spaces clear (do an extra half-hour blitz weekly).
- Relocate anything that has gone astray back to its proper home.
- Enlist the help of everyone who lives with you – allocated chores work wonders.
- Clear out your mailbox last thing on a Friday.
- Action the documents in the in- and out-trays on your desk.

Monthly

- Do filing and admin, such as your monthly banking and bill payments.
- Check or make appointments that are outstanding.
- Clear out your purse or wallet and handbag or briefcase.
- Empty the kitchen cupboards of foodstuffs that need eating or tossing out.
- Clear the hotspot collection point created in the kitchen where you dump keys, post and handbags, for example.

Every six months

- Clear out and update your clothes and current look.
- Do the same for linen and towels.
- Get all your filing and admin 100% up to date, including your tax and financials.
- Clear out that 'dumping drawer' you may have created in the living room.

Annually

- Clear out the spare room, garage and other general dumping grounds.
- Tackle the garden: weed, re-pot and prune, for example.
- Take another look at your books, magazines and CDs.
- Evaluate the general items in your home such as furniture, soft furnishings and dishes to check they still appeal to you and energize you. Sometimes just altering a few cushions and throws can revitalize your home.

Keeping your life a little more organized and structured will have untold positive effects on all areas of your life. If you spend time clearing regularly, you will never again have to embark on an intense program. It is so much easier to keep on giving yourself every opportunity to be clutter free, always timeously letting go of things that no longer serve you.

I wish you well as you embark on the rest of the year, and look forward to being able to help you with another area of your life one day.

Dear Kate,

So my journey with you started almost a year ago to the day ... An innocent Women's Day breakfast attended with my mum, and there you were as one of the speakers. I had seen you on TV a few times prior to that, and every time I did, I thought how wonderful it would be to meet you and get someone like you to assist me in getting my life back on track.

I had been on such an insanely hard ride with work, family and well just with life ... and then you came along. I met you for a one-on-one coaching session, and in the two-plus hours that I spent with you my life just exploded into awesomeness!

I then did your **Spring-clean your life** *28-day process and my whole space transformed into a place of joy, serenity, calmness, happiness and I don't just mean for me. My family felt it too. There was a sense of 'everything just coming together' and that for me was the most amazing thing ever.*

My home became livable again, after being a space that was totally full of bad memories of past hurts and things that I thought had meaning to me, but instead just held me back in a space I was fighting so hard to get out of!

So, thank you for the amazing work you do, for the incredible light that you shine into the darkest of spaces and for the hand you hold out to those of us that think we may be alone.

Much love,
Nicole Philipps

(Nicole has since become my most valuable asset and works as my virtual assistant, as well as for some of my clients who need her help. She is the most incredible proof of letting go and living large!)

Hi Kate

I just wanted to thank you again for helping me. I've struggled with my weight for some six months now and although I needed to lose just 3 kg, the effort of losing it has weighed me down. I felt a failure, suffered continuous migraines because I am intolerant of the foods that were adding the weight, not forgetting the guilt and anger at my failure to do something 'so simple'. In one session, we discovered my payoff, the fact that I don't nurture myself, plus you taught me 'Tapping' and other skills, which I practice daily. I have already dropped a little below my goal weight, feel good about myself – no, extraordinarily **proud** *of myself, the headaches have halved and my clothes* are already looking better. So thank you, thank you, thank you – as we continue together to help me master all this stuff. Please feel free to use this letter of reference, even on your website. Thank you so, so, so very much again.

Karen Milner

I was just going through the motions of buying a house, no excitement, it was just a place to live in. I was miserable in this house for nine months since I bought it, and made up my mind to 'get rid of it'. Kate started me on her **Shift your property** course. I could not believe, from day one, the emotions I had cropped up inside, that I first had to let go of, in order to recognize my house and what it meant to me. With clearing out the emotional and physical clutter, my spirits lifted every day as I worked on the course. I changed my mindset about the house and, as it became cleaner and prettier, I fell in love with it for the first time. Now I feel like buying my own house. I am so in love with it. Thank you, Kate, for opening my eyes, and sorry to the prospective buyer. Although I did not financially 'sell' my house, there's no denying it, Kate. Your system works!

Radia Berry

Hello Kate

What I liked about your program was the step-by-step approach – it was practical and manageable and therefore easier to absorb and deal with. Your way of putting things across was very sympathetic – again easier to 'hear' something and deal with it.

Your program was all-encompassing, with all areas of life, which I liked as well.

Thanks and good luck and let me know when the book is out because I can think of some people I would like to buy it for and not just myself.

Wishing you all the best, which you really deserve.

Kind regards,

Jen

Kate

Spring-clean your life was most useful in tidying up my living space and also helped de-clutter my brain. My work became more efficient and generally I felt rejuvenated. I look forward to reading your book and well done on being commissioned to write one.

Tina

Hello all

After relatively large home renovations, I was left feeling so dissatisfied. All I wanted to do was sell my home ... Remember, this was a house I absolutely loved and wanted badly. Hubby kept saying 'no' to the sale. Thank goodness. After much deliberation and watching one of the shows on **Oprah**, I decided to find a 'house de-clutterer' and up came the name of Kate Emmerson: Life Coach. I made contact, found out what she was all about ... and what the exercise would cost and then sat and did nothing! For a very long three months. All the while feeling more and more discontented. After returning from a short holiday, the wheels were, once again, set in motion. Kate arrived to do, what I thought, my home spring-cleaning! Ha! The joke was on me ...

In came this little dynamo ... Not only did she spring-clean my home but she cleared so much clutter from my head too! The journey and, believe me, it most certainly is a journey, began. No relaxing ride, initially tough. First three days my body went into revolt mode. Aches in places I never knew of anymore. Gut upset – the lot. The more I cleared, the worse it became. Even the family got scared, very scared; I was beginning to change! Then came the 'wanting to cry thing'.

By the next week I felt as if I could really breathe for the first time in years. The feeling of freedom I experienced just letting go of goods and thoughts and ideas that no longer served me was amazing and liberating! I made a bit of money back by selling some stuff to an organization and the rest was donated to Breach, a very worthy organization that helps others less fortunate. They willingly fetch anything you're prepared to part with. Amazing group of people. Having crazy, bubbly and oh-so-cheerful Kate in my life for two whole weeks was brilliant. I think she could make the most miserable person on earth happy. She did most of the heavy work, thank goodness that she's young and able – I don't think my old bones could stand the pace. She finally left and I have to say a huge **thank you for showing me how to regain my freedom and teaching me how to breathe properly and just simply be happy & true to myself.**

For all you did for me, from the bottom of my heart, once again, **thank you!** Much love and see you one day in the near future.

Beverley

We called in Kate and her team because we had reached a stage where we could not clear the clutter ourselves, without conflict. Before we started, we felt claustrophobic, excited and a little nervous. Halfway through, it felt messier than it had ever been, [but we felt] excited and by the end liberated. We now have the ability to keep things under control and want to be in the house, instead of wanting to close the doors to hide untidy rooms. It was also hard for different reasons for the family – Celia: getting rid of my thin clothes; Rachie: feeling like it was a bit out of control; Phil: inability to have coffee every five minutes; but it was easy having someone to clean/wipe/sort so that I could make decisions quickly. Kate and her two helpers spent two days with our family of four (and our two helpers). We emptied, sorted, cleaned, threw out, found long-lost items, packed back, and defied physics by going from chaos to order.

Entropy lost!

It was easy to sort because we had so many people to clean and assist us. We just uttered the words 'don't want' and the item was whisked to the charity pile or the 'to sell' area. 'Keep' meant that it was sorted, categorized and packed in the most suitable, accessible area. Of course, there were those items that were sentimental, and Kate's advice for them was also sage. We kept many of them, but are treating them with the dignity they deserve. We now have empty cupboards, space to dust **around** objects, and an incredible feeling of lightness.

The Haupt Family

At the start, I felt calm; halfway – overwhelmed, methinks; and by the end – blown away by the result, but exhausted. I could not wait to shower and wash it all away. Monday I woke feeling good, but as the day progressed I felt so heavy, body ached, head ached, nauseous, could hardly get myself together. But now I feel fantastic. I keep opening the cupboards to admire it all ... I do feel lighter and more free! No longer concerned who opens my cupboards!

Strangely enough and totally unexpected, the hardest part was the linen ... letting it go. I still had duvet covers from when duvets first came to SA! Okay, I hear you laughing ... No, it was not in the Dark Ages :-). The easiest part was not having to pack it back into the cupboards myself. That in itself was such a blessing, everything in order and in its place. Kate handled the job with love and respect for me, my feelings and my 'things'.

Kate, I can't believe anyone now would want to live with that kind of clutter holding on to all the new things that could be waiting to come in. Having recently been retrenched, it was money well spent. An investment in my future and closure on the past. Will keep you in the loop as to how it progresses.

Love and light and an abundance of blessings ...
Tracey Leppan

And just four months later, Tracey had packed up her life and moved far north to be with her new partner and says this …

> **Hellooooo!** Life here is amazing, almost enchanted between us! Am so very, very happy, darling, very happy and so is he.
>
> I can scarcely believe how well we get on now we are living together. The clutter work helped change my life and move here. I also find that I am no longer bound by material stuff, although it has taken a while.
>
> Tracey Leppan

Need I say more?

FURTHER READING

Branson, Richard. *Screw it, Let's do it* (Virgin Books, 2010).

Canfield, Jack. *The Success Principles* (HarperCollins Publishers, 2005).

Ferriss, Tim. *The 4-hour Work Week* (Crown Publishers, 2007).

Harrold, Fiona. *Be Your own Life Coach* (Hodder & Stoughton, 2000).

Hay, Louise. *You can heal your life* (Hay House, 1985).

Hendrix, Harville. *Getting the love you want* (Harper Perennial, 1991).

Hendrix, Harville. *Keeping the love you find* (Pocket Books, 1995).

Hicks, Esther and Jerry. *The Vortex* (Hay House, 2009).

Kingston, Karen. *Clear your clutter with Feng Shui* (Piatkus, 1998).

Kingston, Karen. *Creating sacred space with Feng Shui* (Piatkus, 1996).

Lerner, Harriet. *The Dance of Anger* (Perennial Currents: 20th Anniversary Edition, May 2005)

Lerner, Harriet. *The Dance of Intimacy* (William Morrow Paperbacks: Reprint edition, March 1990).

Linn, Denise. *Soul Coaching* (Hay House, 2003).

Myss, Caroline. *Anatomy of the Spirit* (Three Rivers Press, 1997).

Myss, Caroline. *Why People don't Heal and how they Can* (Three Rivers Press, 1988).

Ruiz, Don Miguel. *The Four Agreements* (Amber-Allen Publishing, 1997).

Ruiz, Don Miguel. *The Mastery of Love* (Amber-Allen Publishing, 1999).

Walsh, Peter. *It's all too much* (Free Press, 2007).

Williams, Nick. *Resisting Your Soul.* (Nick Williams, 2011).

Williams, Nick. *The Work We Were Born to Do* (Element Books, 1999).

REVIEWS

"Kate shares immediate, doable, straightforward tips on how to liberate your life and yourself from being controlled and restricted by too much stuff, around you and inside you!"

Dorianne Cara Weil "Dr. D" Radio and TV Talk Show Host

"The fantastic balance of useful information, anecdotes and straightforward easy to follow practical guidelines ensures the reader will follow the processes through to the end and achieve an enhanced life, as a result."

Dr. Colin La Grange

"Not only is *Clear you clutter* a book from which you will profit, you'll also want to give it as a gift to those you hope success upon."

Timothy Maurice Webster, Author

"Kate's approachable, direct and conversational style is inviting and like a friend, she guides the reader through every phase, gently and sometimes firmly leading the way to a lighter and more expansive space."

Bonita Nuttall, TV Host and Keynote Speaker

"This is the BEST book on clutter clearing I have ever read … Simply brilliant, brilliantly simple. I love it!"

Fiona Harrold, Best-selling Author, Life Coach

"Kate shares immediate, doable, straightforward tips on how to liberate your life and yourself from being controlled and restricted by too much stuff, around you and inside you!"

Dorianne Cara Weil "Dr. D" Radio and TV Talk Show Host

"[*Clear your clutter*] is light and very inspirational – a must-have in every home. What we loved most about the book is that it is not just about de-cluttering your home but, more importantly, it's about de cluttering your personal and physical life."

Isarae and Bernard Seeff, WPO Chair 2012/13

"Love, love, love this book! ... I'm also buying it for all my office colleagues, friends and family ..."

Florence Niemann, The Fountainhead (Pty) Ltd

"The bible says its more blessed to give than to receive, yet we still find ourselves in a world obsessed with having 'more' – which makes Kate's no-quibble approach to clutter, all the more refreshing – not to mention practical proof that less is more."

Dr Michael Mol, Executive Producer

"Thinking that this book would not have much bearing on my life I settled down and began reading – and here it is, even if you think you may not need it, trust me, you will want it. You will want to embrace the practical steps Kate advises in her no-nonsense yet gentle approach which is always sprinkled with a good dash of humor ... It's a delight to read and ... empowering, even for a simple gardener like me!"

Tanya Visser, Magazine Editor, TV Presenter, Gardening Guru

"This book is a Life Changer. It's about so much more than having a pretty living room. It's about letting go, about being courageous, about having faith ..."

Natasha Sutherland, Author, Actress and Motivational Speaker

"If you have ever had any kind of resistance to keeping your space exactly that, a space, then Kate's words will brightly and swiftly sweep you up. Her clarity and practical tools will liberate your body, mind, heart and house from what stops, blocks and hinders you in life."

Tiamara Williams, President Inspiring Lives Global Change Maker, TV host, Author

"Beware! This book will set you off on a spring-cleaning frenzy way before you've even turned the last page. It's inspiring, galvanizing, and makes so much sense, on so many levels, you'll view your clutter in a wholly different way – and be hard pressed to make a case for it."

Tracy Melass, Media Consultant

Kate has helped me de-clutter and de-stress my life and this book with its practical tips and "how-to's" will certainly help you do the same.

Donna McCallum, the Fairy Godmother

"Filled with insight into the psychological factors surrounding clutter and step-by-step advice that will take you on a practical journey to actually doing it and clearing your clutter, [Clear your clutter] will guide you to fulfill your own destiny."

Fiona Davern, Executive Editor Destiny Magazine: Features

"It is impossible to read [Clear your clutter] and not move something, give something away or throw something out! Read Kate's clutter clearing manifesto and her definition of clutter ("anything that no longer serves you") will sit on your shoulder as an inspirational bird, tweeting at you to TURF."

Natalie Uren, Mentor

Lightning Source UK Ltd.
Milton Keynes UK
UKHW05f1857120318
319326UK00005B/404/P